The Freelance Fairytale

How to Create Your Happy Ever After

Lisa Slater

Make Your Copy Count Ltd

www.makeyourcopycount.com

ISBN 978-1-7391731-1-1 (print)

ISBN 978-1-7391731-0-4 (ebook edition)

The Freelance Fairytale

Once upon a time, there was a hardworking, talented individual who was tired of the traditional nine to five.

They wanted more freedom, more flexibility and more money. They wanted to work for themselves, not for somebody else.

And so, one day, they left the safety and security of a full-time salary and embarked on an adventure into the freelance world.

News spread of this freelancer's venture, and wonderful clients appeared from across the land, paying the freelancer handsomely for their work.

Within weeks, the freelancer was spending their days working on stuff they enjoyed and projects they were passionate about.

They had the freedom, flexibility, and money they had always dreamed of, and they lived happily ever after.

The end.

Ah – if only it were that simple, eh?

Like me, you probably hit the freelance life with high hopes and bags of enthusiasm.

You're amazing at what you do and have loads of experience, skills, and knowledge, so it'll be easy to get clients, right?

Until it's not.

That's the problem with fairytales – they give us false expectations of what life will be like. They teach us that as long as you're a good person, everything will work out perfectly in the end.

Wouldn't it be great if real life actually worked that way?

And it doesn't help that social media is full of fairy stories.

Freelancers who make six figures a week working from the beach.

Freelancers who have gone from living on the streets to living in mansions and owning private jets.

Freelancers who have built and scaled business empires that now turn over millions of dollars a year.

We're suckers for a rags-to-riches story. They give us hope.

But sometimes, hope isn't enough.

Finger crossing doesn't make clients appear or put cash in the bank.

Don't get me wrong, there are some real-life fairytale endings out there. But they are the exception, not the norm. The reality is most small businesses don't make it.

And the freelancers who do make it past one year, three years, or five years aren't all sitting on the beach with a laptop or making money while they sleep.

Some are ticking along nicely, not making millions, but making a very comfortable living. Others are stuck in a feast and famine cycle, not knowing whether they'll earn enough to pay their bills from one month to the next. Many fall somewhere in between.

Freelance life can be tough – really tough.

But it doesn't have to be.

You can have your happy ever after.

You just have to put a bit of work in first.

And I'm here to help you do it – think of me as your fairy godmother.

Contents

INTRODUCTION

The tale of the frustrated freelancer

If you're reading this book, you likely have one or more of the following frustrations:

- You aren't attracting enough clients
- You aren't attracting the right leads
- You are always busy but aren't earning as much as you'd like
- You're trapped in a feast and famine cycle
- You've followed all the usual marketing advice but nothing works
- You're on every social media platform but rarely get enquiries
- You have clients you don't enjoy working with
- You don't get enough of the work you love
- You take on low-paying work just to cover the bills
- You are constantly chasing invoices
- You keep getting ghosted by people

These are all common problems freelancers face, and there are plenty more on top. But the good news is they are all problems that can be solved.

And that's why I'm writing this book. I'm going to be for you the person I wish I'd had by my side in the early years of my business.

Someone who understands what it's like but can also give you practical, actionable advice to help you move forward.

From frustrated to fulfilled

This book is about you, but you probably want some reassurance that I know what I'm talking about, so let me introduce myself very quickly.

I got my first copywriting client in 2014 while still working full-time. In 2016, I went all-in on my business and quit the nine to five.

The first two years of self-employment were exciting. I did what most new business owners do and jumped at every "opportunity".

But by year three, I felt stuck in a rut. I made enough to pay my mortgage and cover my bills, but I was experiencing almost all the problems I mentioned earlier. And I was falling out of love with my business.

I was a frustrated freelancer.

For a while, I kept plodding along, waiting for that pivotal moment. The moment when everything would click into place, and I'd have the business I always wanted. I worked hard, was good at what I did, and got great feedback – it would all pay off eventually, right?

Then one day, I realised if I wanted things to change, I had to be the one to change them. I'd love to tell you there was a specific turning point – one particular thing that sparked it all. But there wasn't.

I just decided I wasn't happy with my business anymore, and I had to change things. So I did.

It didn't happen overnight. I didn't wake up one morning and suddenly have the business I wanted just because I wanted it.

I implemented lots of little changes. And I kept an open mind.

I stopped saying "that won't work for me" or "I can't do that in my business", and started trying new ways of working.

I increased my prices, changed my services, started saying no, employed and outsourced, and built a business that worked on my terms.

I got help. I sought out people who had achieved the things I wanted to achieve and learnt from them. I started working with a mentor.

In 2020, I began offering one-to-one marketing consultations. A year later, I launched a copywriting training and mentoring programme.

But although people were initially coming to me for copywriting or marketing advice, it often turned out they needed help with their business in general. Advice on things like pricing and processes, enquiry handling and sales, and how to say no.

And that's how I transitioned from copywriter to business mentor.

I'd been where they had been. I'd built a business from nothing, and I understood the challenges, the frustrations, the things that get in the way.

Most importantly, I'd figured out how to overcome those challenges and build a business that makes me happy.

I created my happy ever after.

Now I'm going to help you create yours.

Forget magic beans

Remember the story of Jack and the Beanstalk?

Young Jack was sent to sell the family cow and returned with magic beans instead of money.

His furious mother hurled the beans out the window, and off they went to bed.

Luckily for Jack, his magic beans paid off and grew into a giant beanstalk, leading him to the giant's castle and a wealth of gold.

It's a lovely story, but unfortunately, there are no magic beans in business.

There is no silver bullet, secret sauce, or fool-proof formula to success. It doesn't stop people from looking though.

Everyone wants 'magic beans' – something that will change their fortunes overnight.

It's why so many people fall for get-rich-quick schemes. You know the ones – how to make six figures a day from the beach by doing this one thing.

The only people making money from those schemes are the people selling them – if it really were as easy as they say it is, everyone would be doing it.

They are selling magic beans.

And there's no such thing as magic beans.

So if you're reading this book hoping I'll give you a quick and easy fix to your business, stop reading now. The fix is simple but not easy – it involves doing some work.

How quickly you get the results you want will depend on where you are now, where you want to be, and how willing you are to do what you need to do.

Are you up for the challenge?

Good. Let's get started.

Part one: Once upon a time

Your story starts here

If you're a frustrated freelancer, coach, consultant, or service provider, this book is for you.

It's based on stuff I do in my business. Stuff I know works. Stuff that has helped me create a happy life.

You can take some of it, none of it, or all of it and use it in your business – it's entirely up to you.

I don't expect you to agree with everything I say. But I do ask that you keep an open mind.

Be prepared to do things that might not feel comfortable at first, and be ready to make changes.

I can give you all the advice in the world – tell you exactly what you need to do – but if you aren't prepared to implement anything I tell you, you won't get results.

This book won't transform your business – only you can do that. Are you ready?

Emperor's new clothes

Do you know the story of the Emperor's New Clothes?

Two swindlers take advantage of a wealthy, vain emperor. They pretend to be weavers and tell him they can make him the most exquisite outfit, but it will be invisible to anyone who is stupid or incompetent.

The emperor falls for their pitch, and they get to work making his new clothes. At various stages, they show off their work to the emperor and his advisors.

Of course, neither the emperor nor his advisors can see the invisible outfit, but none of them wants to look stupid or incompetent, so they all pretend they can see it.

When the time comes for the emperor to wear his new outfit, he still can't see it. But rather than admit he can't see it, he joins the weavers in admiring the beauty and quality of the garments. His officials don't want to appear stupid or incompetent, so they pretend to admire it too.

The weavers make a big show of helping the emperor into his outfit, and off he goes to impress his loyal subjects with his lavish new clothes.

Nobody wants to look foolish, so they all keep quiet about the fact the emperor is parading the streets naked. It's only when a child starts to laugh and point that people realise the emperor has been taken for a complete mug.

He was too concerned about **looking** stupid to realise he was **being** stupid.

That's the problem with ego. It often gets in the way of common sense and good decision-making.

Rather than admit things aren't working, it's easier to keep up a charade. Pretend everything is ok.

But if you aren't getting the clients you want, if you aren't doing work you enjoy, if your business isn't where you want it to be, you need to admit something isn't working.

Don't be like the emperor. Don't keep parading the streets naked, too proud to admit there's a problem.

Don't keep doing the same thing and expecting new results

It's perfectly ok to admit something isn't getting the results you want if you are prepared to do something about it. But realising something isn't getting results and then continuing to do it anyway is stupid.

Imagine you put your hand in a jar to grab a coin. You make a fist around the coin and try to pull it out. But now you've made a fist, your hand no longer fits back through the opening.

What would you do? Keep trying to force your hand out, even though it clearly won't fit, or let go of the coin and try getting it out another way?

It's the same in business. If what you are doing isn't working, you need to try something else. If you aren't prepared to change your approach, your results won't change.

And just because you've always done something a certain way doesn't mean you have to keep doing it that way.

Take the emotion out of it

Around ten years ago, one of my friends discovered her partner was cheating on her. They split up, but they both wanted to keep the house.

My friend spoke to a solicitor, and the solicitor said, "take the emotion out of it."

She advised my friend to let go of anger, pride and attachment to the house. View the situation rationally – would the cost of fighting for it be worth it, or would it be better to take a pay-off and walk away?

As it turned out, my friend's ex couldn't get a mortgage for the house by himself, so my friend got to keep it.

But the solicitor's advice – "take the emotion out of it" – has always stuck with me.

All too often, ego or pride get in the way of being objective.

Sometimes it's hard to let go and walk away. It's hard to admit we were wrong about something or have been doing things wrong. To admit we made a mistake, are failing at something, or are giving up. Nobody likes to admit defeat.

You often see people embroiled in pointless arguments on social media because they are so determined to have the last word and prove they are right. Why are they wasting their energy?

Or you have friends who stay in terrible relationships, hoping it will get better because they've already invested five years of their life. How do you convince them that walking away after five years is better than wasting another five?

And you see freelancers and business owners pumping time or money into marketing that doesn't work because they don't want to admit everything they have invested so far has amounted to nothing.

I used to be terrible at admitting I was wrong. But I realised very early in business you cannot let your ego get in the way of sensible decisions.

If I spend money or time on something that doesn't work, I walk away. I cut my losses. I don't waste more time or money on it.

Know when to cut your losses

Walking away with nothing to show for your time, effort or money can be hard.

It's like when a gambler loses a little money and keeps doubling down to try and win it back.

With each new bet, they are trying to recoup their losses, but the more they lose, the harder it becomes to walk away. All they need is that one big win.

But what if that big win never comes, and they lose everything?

Business owners do this all the time.

They don't want to admit they've lost money, wasted time, or put effort into the wrong things.

Rather than cutting their losses and walking away, they keep investing more time, money, or effort, hoping their investment will eventually pay off.

Forget what you've already put in and be realistic – are you ever going to get the desired result if you don't change your approach? If the answer is no, cut your losses.

If you started walking down a road and realised it was taking you in the wrong direction, you wouldn't carry on walking. You'd turn around, walk back the way you came, and find the right road instead.

It's the same with your business – if it's not heading in the right direction, don't just keep going, or you won't end up where you want to be.

Take accountability for your success (and failures)

It doesn't matter how far you've gone in one direction – you can always change direction.

If your business isn't making you happy, do something about it.

Even if it means sacking all your clients and starting from scratch. Even if it means doing things you previously said were rubbish or giving up on things you once swore by.

It's ok to change your mind about things. It's ok to see things from a new perspective. It's ok to admit something isn't working.

But only you can make the change. Only you can take back control of your business and move it in the direction you want it to go.

You might not want to hear this – I know I didn't – but the challenges in your business are your fault.

If you are getting low-paying clients, it's because you agree to work with low-paying clients.

If you work too many hours, it's because you are taking on too much work.

If you aren't getting enough clients, it's because your sales and marketing process isn't up to scratch.

It's a hard pill to swallow. But if you accept it and deal with it, you can remove the barriers that have been holding you back and achieve the things you want to achieve.

The people who have achieved "success" aren't part of some secret society. They are people who have done what they needed to do. You can do that too.

You are responsible for your happiness – nobody else.

Those stories you tell yourself can be rewritten. Those negative comments people make can be ignored. That nagging self-doubt can be overcome.

What is success?

Success is different for everyone. Some people see being number one in their field as success. But not everyone can be number one, so is number two unsuccessful? Is the second-best footballer in the world unsuccessful?

Some people base success on money. But how much money is enough? A million? A billion? How much do you need in your account to be deemed successful?

Is success a big house and a nice car? A business with 100 employees? Being able to retire at 45?

How do you define success?

I define success as happiness. To me, being successful is having a happy life. And that's why this book is called "how to create your happy ever after".

It's not called "how to get rich quick" or "how to build a business empire" because those things might not be the things that make you happy.

That's not to say this book won't teach you how to do those things if that's what you want. But is that what you want?

It's too easy to get distracted by other people's definitions of success.

"You need to make six figures"

"You need to make seven figures"

"You need to scale"

"You need to build a big team"

"You need a business that works without you"

"You need to create passive income"

"You need to create a sellable business"

You don't "need" to do any of those things if those things won't make you happy.

Personally, I just want to earn enough money to travel the world with my husband, live comfortably, and treat my nieces and nephews whenever I can. I want to be able to enjoy life now and save enough so that one day I can stop working (if I want to).

I don't want to work eighty-hour weeks, building an empire. I want enough flexibility to take a week or two off to have a proper holiday. I want to be able to meet a friend for lunch on a weekday or spend a day in the garden when it's sunny – I don't want to be chained to my desk.

That's my happy ever after, and I'm living it.

Things might change, but for now, I'm right where I want to be.

I attract clients I like working with and do work I enjoy. I earn enough money and have enough flexibility to live the lifestyle I want. I'm happy. And I want you to be happy too.

But you need to decide what success and happiness mean to you. What does your version of happy ever after look like?

Invest now or live for today?

When it comes to money and time, people have different views.

Do you make sacrifices now to have the future you want? Or do you enjoy life now because you don't know how long you've got?

I know people who go without treats and luxuries so they can save all their money for retirement. And I know people who love a good splurge because "you only live once".

I know people who miss out on social events and holidays because they invest all their time into building a sellable business that will allow them to retire in ten years.

And I know people who work just enough to earn what they need because they chose self-employment to give themselves more free time.

There is no right or wrong. You could invest all your time and money into your future for the next five years and then die a year later. Or you could live for the moment and never be able to retire.

I try and create balance. I work hard, and I put a little money into a pension and savings. But I don't sit at my desk until the early hours of the morning, miss out on seeing friends, or go without holidays.

You need to decide what your priorities are and build your business around them.

Let's talk about money

The way people view money varies dramatically – some people view it as a necessary evil, some view it as plain evil, others think it's the answer to everything.

But money isn't good or bad – it's just something that exists.

You don't need money to make you happy, but you do need money to pay for a roof over your head, food in your belly, and clothes on your back.

And it's not greedy to want a comfortable lifestyle or financial security.

It's not greedy to want to be able to eat properly and heat our homes.

It's not greedy to want nice things in life.

It's ok to want to earn money.

Don't focus on figures

Having financial goals is sensible, but don't base them on monetary figures.

"I want to make six figures a month"

"I want to make seven figures a year"

"I want to be a billionaire by the time I'm 50"

You won't wake up full of joy the day your bank account hits a million pounds.

All that will happen if you hit your target is you'll want more.

And unless you know how to use that cash to make you happy, it's pointless.

Think about what you want from life and base your financial goals around that.

Me and my husband love travelling, visiting new places, seeing new countries, and trying new things. But to do those things, we need money.

If it's a big house you want, you need money to buy it. If you want to send your children to a private school or support them financially while they're at university, you need money.

If you want to retire at 50 and travel the world in a motorhome, you need money.

Even if you simply want enough to cover your bills and buy a few treats, you still need money.

So figure out what you want and make it your goal to earn enough money to achieve it.

Don't make money your priority

Earning the money you need to buy the things you want shouldn't mean sacrificing your happiness, neglecting your loved ones, or compromising your integrity.

I've never heard of anyone getting to the end of their life and saying:

"I wish I'd spent less time with my family and friends"

"I wish I'd spent less time enjoying myself"

"I wish I'd spent more time working"

"I wish I'd screwed more people over to get rich"

Making money shouldn't make you miserable. You don't have to put up with horrible clients for the sake of a few quid.

You don't have to miss important family events because you want that extra bit of cash this week.

And you certainly shouldn't be scamming people out of their money because you want a shortcut to success.

View money as nice to have, not need to have – don't make it the focus of your happiness.

Action time: What does your happy ever after look like?

This probably isn't the first business book you've ever read, in which case, you'll be familiar with the idea of goal setting.

If you don't know what you're working toward, how do you know if you're heading in the right direction?

So this is your first task – work out what your happy ever after looks like.

If you could wake up tomorrow in your dream business, what would it look like? What kind of clients would you have? What kind of work would you be doing (if any)?

If you only want to think about the short term, let's focus on that. Where do you want your business to be a year from now? How much do you want to be earning? How many hours do you want to be working?

I know plenty of freelancers who aren't chasing seven-figure turnovers. They simply want to do the thing they love every day and make enough to live on.

They aren't interested in creating assets or teams or passive income streams. They just want good clients who pay them what they are worth.

But if you do have a longer-term goal, what does it look like? Do you want to build a team? Create a sellable business? Earn enough to retire in ten years?

Be honest. Don't just set a goal you think you should have based on what "everyone else" is doing. What do you want from life? If you don't want to be a billionaire, that's fine. If you do, that's fine too.

This book is about creating your version of happy ever after. I can only show you how to do that if you know what it looks like.

I'm not saying you have to have it nailed down, and it doesn't have to be the ultimate goal – it can be the goal for now. But you need to be working towards something.

Don't skip this step. Write it down. You don't have to share it with anyone, but it'll help you stay focused if you know what you're working towards.

What does happy ever after mean to you?

What does 'happy ever after' look like?

The story so far: Part one summary

Key takeaways:

- You are responsible for taking control of your business – nobody else can do it for you.
- Don't let ego or emotion get in the way of sensible business decisions – know when to let go and walk away.
- Success is different for everyone – only you can determine what success looks like for you.
- Don't make your financial goals about monetary figures – make them about the lifestyle you want.
- Never compromise your integrity or values for the sake of money.

Action points:

- Decide what happy ever after means to you.

Coming up next:

- How to stay on course to your happy ever after.

Part two: Steer clear of the toxic swamp

Stick to the path

In the story of Little Red Riding Hood, Little Red is given strict instructions by her mother to stick to the path all the way to Grandma's house.

'Stick to the path' is good advice for your business too.

You've set your goal – your happy ever after – now you've got to get there.

But, just like Little Red, you need to navigate your way through the forest, and the forest is full of distractions.

Don't get side-tracked. Stick to the path and get to grandma's house.

In other words, don't take on clients you don't want, don't take on projects you can't do or won't enjoy, and don't get lured into doing stuff that doesn't add value to your business or move you closer to your goal.

Saying 'no' isn't always easy but saying 'yes' isn't always right

There's a Richard Branson quote that gets thrown around all too often:

"If somebody offers you an amazing opportunity, but you are not sure you can do it, say yes – then learn how to do it later!"

But while you have to do some 'learning on the job' when you start out, it doesn't mean you should agree to everything.

If something is outside your area of expertise (and learning how to do it won't benefit you long-term), don't do it. Stick to what you're good at.

And stick to what you enjoy. Just because you can do something doesn't mean you should.

What's the point of taking on projects you don't feel comfortable with? You'll only spend your time second-guessing yourself or resenting the work.

You don't have to agree to everything.

And you certainly don't have to agree to unpaid or low-paying work.

If someone asks you to do free work in return for 'exposure' or on the promise of more work, run a mile. These 'opportunities' rarely turn into paid work, and exposure doesn't pay the bills.

Stick to your guns regarding price – don't discount just because someone asks nicely. If they don't see the value in your skills, do you really want to work with them?

Turning away work, even if it is low paying, can feel scary. But think about it this way – how would your full-paying clients feel if they knew you were giving others the same service for free or at a discount? It seems a little unfair.

And I can tell you from experience the clients who aren't prepared to pay your full rates almost always end up being the most difficult to work with. Why should they pay less and get more of your time and energy?

They shouldn't. Your price is your price, and you've set your price for a reason.

Giving value doesn't mean working for free

"Give value. Givers gain. Give. Give. Give. If you help other people, they will be more inclined to help you."

I'm sure you've heard people giving this advice. And to an extent, it's true.

But if you're constantly giving away free advice, doing free calls, and meeting random strangers for coffee to 'explore opportunities', you end up overworked and underpaid.

Filling your days with calls and meetings might feel productive, and helping people does feel good. But if you're not being paid for all that time you're giving to others, you will be busy but not profitable.

There's a fine line between using your expertise as a marketing tool and working for free. And it's a line that's easy to blur.

I am a massive fan of content marketing – it's a great way of building trust and credibility. I say go all in on blogs, videos, social posts and lead magnets. Give value, share tips, make your content useful.

But don't work for free.

Don't 'jump on a quick call' with people or let people 'quickly pick your brain'.

Giving your time for free to provide bespoke advice rarely leads to a good outcome. In most cases, one of three things will happen:

They'll ignore your advice because it is not what they wanted to hear, and they didn't pay for it, so they won't value it.

They'll implement your suggestions themselves or find someone to do it on the cheap (and they probably won't get the results you would have got them).

They'll keep coming back with 'one more question' or another 'quick request' with no intention of ever buying.

None of these scenarios gives you any return on your investment of time. You might feel nice about helping people, but you aren't going to feel so great when you go out of business because you aren't making any money.

The more of your time, knowledge, and skill you give away for free, the less people value it. It's sad but true.

If you don't value your time and expertise, other people won't value it either.

Stop kissing frogs

A big part of your happy ever after is going to be getting the right clients, but you have to kiss a few frogs before you find your prince, right?

Actually, you don't. You don't have to entertain any frog-snogging in business.

In other words, you don't have to put up with less than desirable prospects or crappy customers in the hope some of them will turn into your dream clients.

I'm in the fortunate position where I can be selective about who I work with. But it's not because I'm rolling in cash. It's because my marketing attracts the right people. And that means if the wrong people do happen to get in touch, I can politely decline their advances.

If you're getting bad vibes from a potential client, don't be afraid to tell them you don't think you're a good fit. You don't have to justify it or explain your reasons.

Remember, your goal is to create your happy ever after, and you won't be happy working with people who:

- Want you to jump through hoops to win their business
- Expect you to work for free or for 'exposure'
- Ask for a proposal, then disappear without a trace

- Aren't prepared to pay your going rate
- Don't value what you do
- Micro-manage you
- Make unreasonable demands on your time
- Expect you to drop everything for them when they need you
- Don't get back to you with information you need
- Don't pay on time

These types of prospects and clients are frogs, and they rarely turn into princes.

And if the fact they'll make you miserable isn't reason enough to run a mile from these frog clients, think how unfair you are being to your good clients by taking them on.

How will you focus on completing a good client's project to a high standard when you're distracted by a demanding frog?

Why should a good client get less of your time and energy because a frog is getting more than their fair share?

You should avoid taking frogs on in the first place, but if you do end up with one (or you are currently working with one), you need to take action. You don't have to be rude about it. Either let the agreement come to a natural end or give notice.

You don't have to explain why, but they might be open to change if you do. Not everyone realises they are being difficult. Perhaps you just need to set some boundaries.

On the other hand, they might just be an arsehole, and if they are, you need to move on.

Turning away paying customers might sound scary, especially if you are starting out or only just making enough money to get by. But keeping them is detrimental to your business.

The energy you waste on toxic clients could be put into giving your best clients a better service so they don't go elsewhere, so they recommend you, and so they want to invest in more of your services. Or it could be put into attracting more of the clients you want.

So stop frog-snogging. You don't have to smooch those slimy amphibians to find your dream clients.

Make today the day you put your foot down and stop taking on frogs. You deserve better.

Beware the big bad wolf

Just like Red Riding Hood, you need to beware of the 'big bad wolf'. A big bad wolf is someone who will take you off course and distract you from your goals.

They aren't necessarily trying to sabotage your business – they're just giving terrible advice. And, let's face it, there's a scary amount of bad business advice out there.

Some of it is well-meant but based on nothing but guesswork, some is purposely malicious, and some is just plain toxic.

Here are some of the big bad wolves you should steer clear of.

The echo chambers

Do you want to solve your problem or just feel better about it?

If you want to solve it, don't ask for advice from people with the same problem as you. They can't help you solve it – if they could, they wouldn't have the problem themselves.

All they can do is help you live with the problem. They'll tell you it's part of freelance life, and you just have to learn to accept it. (Spoiler: you don't).

You'll end up in an echo chamber where you all complain about the same thing, agree on how terrible it is, and reassure each other that it's all ok.

It's easy to get sucked into echo chambers. They are comfortable because you all have something in common. But you won't get much in the way of useful advice from people with the same problem as you if they have no idea how to solve it.

And watch out for people operating under the "fake it until you make it" banner. They want to appear successful, even if they aren't.

The problem is they aren't giving advice based on experience. They simply regurgitate the same motivational quotes, inspiring stories, and generic advice they've seen or read elsewhere.

Half the time, they aren't even following the advice they're giving out to others. They'll happily tell you what a great investment outsourcing is, even though they've never outsourced anything themselves.

They'll tell you to invest in experts and pay to get things done properly, but they'll spend their days looking for freebies.

And they'll happily give advice on marketing and sales when they haven't got a clue how to attract clients themselves.

If you want helpful business advice, get it from people who have actually built the kind of business you want.

The self-proclaimed gurus

If you've been in business for more than five minutes, you'll have seen one of these scammers touting their formula for success.

"*I was down and out, on the verge of bankruptcy, and about to lose everything when I suddenly discovered the one secret that turned me into an overnight millionaire. Now I want to share it with you.*"

All you have to do is pay £27 for a training video/webinar/workshop/event (which turns out to be a glorified sales pitch for a £10k mastermind course).

These people are not selling you a solution. They are selling hope. They are selling you magic beans, but as we know, magic beans don't exist.

If a person makes so much money they own five Lamborghinis, a super yacht, and a private jet, why on earth would they be flogging a thirty-quid course on Facebook?

They wouldn't.

You don't see Richard Branson, Bill Gates, or Jeff Bezos making get-rich-quick videos, do you?

Be wary of anyone claiming they can help you build a six-figure business overnight.

If you're thinking of handing over big sums of money to a business coach or guru, do your due diligence. Check whether their claims are legit – can they really help you achieve what they say they can?

The positive thinkers

"*All you have to do is think positive thoughts, and all your dreams will come true. It's all about a positive mindset, laws of attraction, and wanting it bad enough.*"

Bullshit.

This type of advice is toxic. People spouting this crap are basically implying that people fail in business because they don't want success badly enough.

I'm not saying you shouldn't adopt a positive mindset – you absolutely should. But it shouldn't replace action. Self-belief isn't a magic wand.

I'm sorry to burst the bubble, but good things don't happen just because you wish for them. Crossing your fingers won't bring clients to your door. And visualising money will not make it magically appear in your bank.

If you want clients, you have to go out and get them (more on how to do that later).

You can't wish yourself to success. And if you're hoping it'll be that easy, you're in the wrong place. Put this book down, request a refund, and I'll keep my fingers crossed for you that it all works out.

The "hustle and grind" crew

"*Wake up at the crack of dawn, run a marathon while closing a deal, meditate, check your emails, work, work, work, post a motivational video, lift some weights, work through the night, sleep for an hour, and then start all over again.*"

No thanks.

Get up at 4am. Don't get up at 4am. Work eighty hours a week. Work eight hours a week. Meditate after lunch. Take a walk after lunch. Take a nap after lunch.

Do whatever suits you. It's your business and your life.

Just because somebody else got successful by having a strict routine of spinach smoothies for breakfast, not checking emails before 3pm, and running a marathon before every meeting doesn't mean it will work for you.

Routine works for some people and not for others. Find your own formula. And don't put too much stock in the idea that you have to work until you drop if you want to be successful.

Hard work doesn't always translate into success. You can work hard at the wrong things.

If you're filling your week with low-paying work, making just enough to cover the bills, and never finding time to grow your business, you aren't going to create your happy ever after, no matter how hard you're working at it. You're going to be stuck doing low-paying work forever.

There's nothing wrong with working long hours, evenings and weekends if it takes you closer to your happy ever after. But don't feel bad if you don't want to dedicate every waking hour to your business.

The cults

When you enter the world of self-employment, you can easily get sucked into cult-like situations.

It's understandable when you think about it – we're used to being led. As a child, we follow the rules of our parents or guardians. At school, it's our teachers providing authority. And when we get a job, we have bosses.

So when you're suddenly in a world where nobody is making the rules, it's tempting to look for someone to follow.

There are examples of it everywhere you look.

First up, the pyramid schemes disguised as an opportunity to run your own business.

On paper, it's the dream – a ready-made business with amazing products. All you have to do is sell those products. The more you sell, the more you make.

Sounds great until you're expected to build a team – in other words, recruit more people into the pyramid.

Then you have the referral networking groups. You're joining a group of like-minded people who all want to help each other succeed in business.

You have a network of contacts who can connect you with your ideal clients – as long as you play the game, find them referrals in return, and follow the rules of course.

And then there are the 'influencers' and the 'gurus'. They have thousands of adoring followers, all hanging on their every word.

They dish out marketing and business advice based on what worked for them and tell you to ignore anything that doesn't fit their way of doing things.

But here's the thing with pyramid schemes, networking organisations, and your favourite influencers – you don't have to follow them religiously.

If the tactics they promote aren't delivering the results they promised, don't pump more time, money, and energy in.

Take the best bits – the bits most relevant to your business, most aligned with your values, and most likely to help you get results.

I think pyramid schemes should be avoided at all costs. But if you have been sucked into one, you've probably gained a few useful skills. Escape the pyramid scheme and use these skills to set up a real business offering something people actually want.

Networking can be a useful tool – I was part of a networking group for three years and made some great business contacts and friends. But don't make networking your only marketing strategy – you'll be depending on other people to get you results.

And if you're putting more time and effort into networking than running your business, it's time to rethink your approach.

As for influencers? They aren't messiahs. You don't have to worship them and hang on their every word. It's ok to disagree with them now and then, despite what their loyal disciples might believe.

Just because you like someone doesn't mean you have to agree with everything they say or do. There are people I admire and respect, but it doesn't mean I agree with their opinion on everything.

You probably won't agree with everything I say – it doesn't mean the rest of what I say isn't valid.

And just because you don’t like someone doesn’t mean their advice isn't worth listening to.

Be open-minded and think for yourself. It’s ok to gain insight from multiple sources.

You don’t have to follow one leader. You don’t have to subscribe to one business ideology. And you don’t have to blindly follow someone else’s bible.

Feast and famine is not inevitable

Many freelancers, coaches and consultants talk about the feast and famine cycle as though it is inevitable.

It's not.

You might have certain times of the year where your enquiries peak or trough – I'm often a little quieter than usual in August and a little busier around the new year. But these peaks and troughs are manageable.

They aren't the same as the feast and famine cycle where you are overwhelmed with work one month and then wondering whether you'll be able to pay the mortgage the next.

The good news is these cycles can be broken.

You don't have to suffer periods of overwhelm and stress followed by periods of anxiety and panic. Get your money, time, and marketing under control, and you'll see more feasts than famines.

Manage your money

Getting control of your money will help you manage the feast and famine cycle more effectively. You won't get to the point where you have to take on any old project or overload yourself with work just to cover the bills.

Price correctly

If your prices are too low, you will have to take on more work than you should just to earn the money you need to cover your bills.

Let's say you need £4000 per month to cover your personal and business costs – mortgage or rent, bills, car, food, internet, website costs, accountant, IT, etc.

The minimum you need to bill each month is £4000 – that's the minimum. Ideally, you'd want a bit extra towards unexpected costs and luxuries, so let's say £6000 is your target amount.

If you are charging the equivalent of £30 per hour, you have to do 200 billable hours of work per month. In a 30-day month, that works out at between 6 and 7 hours a day. And that's without a day off and without accounting for non-billable work such as admin and marketing.

If you take a week off or have a month where you don't get much work, you'll be playing catch up, working 60, 70, 80 hours or more.

And while it's fine to work long hours, it should be because you choose to, not because you have to.

Get your pricing right, and you won't have to take on every single project that comes your way just to pay the bills.

Create a buffer

The temptation when you have a 'feast' phase is to pay yourself a bit extra and have a few treats, but this can leave you short two months down the line when things go quiet again. That's why I leave any extra money in my business.

I pay myself the same monthly amount even when I exceed my sales targets. This helps me build a buffer so I can still pay myself if I have a below-average month, a month with lots of outgoings, or a month where I go on holiday. Once I have a comfortable buffer, I pay myself a 'bonus'.

Ideally, you want to get to a position where you have enough of a buffer that you could still cover all your bills if you had no billable work for a month (or even longer).

The chances of you getting no billable work are probably slim, but this is a worst-case scenario.

What it means is you don't get to the point of desperation. You aren't so worried about money that you take on low-paying work or start discounting your rates.

The problem with filling your time with discounted work is that you don't have time to go out and get the clients and work you want.

If you hold a little money back each month, you can stand your ground with your prices. And once you've built up a comfortable buffer, you can give yourself a pay rise or treat yourself to a bonus.

Invoice upfront

Unfortunately, not all clients pay their invoices quickly, which can be a real problem if you're relying on that money to pay your bills.

You don't want to spend hours chasing payments for work you completed months ago, especially if you are only just hitting your monthly sales targets. And what will you do if a client decides they aren't going to pay?

Getting paid in advance for your work means you know you have cash in the bank to pay next month's bills. You don't have to scrape the barrel for work to tide you over or take on extra work to cover unpaid invoices.

Manage your time

If you manage your time effectively, you don't have to spend your quieter periods chasing work. You can use them to work on side projects or business development.

Create efficient systems

Even something as simple as having proposal templates can save a significant amount of time. Rather than spending hours writing out the same thing, you take the relevant sections of the prewritten template and then fill in the blanks as needed.

But where you can really make a difference is putting processes in place for managing enquiries to filter out timewasters before you end up on a call or in a meeting with them.

When you're desperate for work, it can seem like a good idea to 'jump on a call' with someone who is 'interested in your services'. While this might occasionally turn into work, it quite often turns out to be a waste of time. They either want to pump you for free advice or get a quote to compare against all their other quotes.

If you have systems to qualify enquiries before you agree to calls, you eliminate this problem. And you can use the time you're not wasting on pointless calls to focus on attracting better leads in the first place.

Make time for marketing even when you are busy

One of the main contributors to the feast and famine cycle is erratic marketing. When freelancers hit a famine phase, they usually have a big push on sales and marketing.

They go to networking events, spend more time on social media, write blog posts, or make videos. They have more time for calls and meetings, following up on emails, and putting together detailed proposals.

All that effort pays off, and they get an influx of work. But now they have so much work they don't have time for all that other stuff. Marketing gets neglected. Calls, emails, and proposals get missed or rushed.

And then, when the busy period is over, they have no more work lined up. So then what happens? There's another mad push on marketing and business development. And round and round the cycle goes.

You need to break the cycle by making time for marketing even when you're busy. Whether you schedule an hour a day or half a day a week, put it in your calendar and treat it as you would a client project – make it a priority.

Use quiet periods to work on your business

If you do find yourself in a quiet phase, use it to your advantage. Don't spend it running around every networking event you can find in the hope you'll bump into someone who needs your help. Use it to work on your marketing and business development.

Use it to create those templates and put effective systems in place. Research new software and review your existing processes.

Use it to work on your marketing. Pre-write a batch of social media posts so you have content prepared for when you're busy again. Update your website or social media profiles.

Use it for personal development. Build on your existing skills or learn new skills. Do refresher courses or familiarise yourself with new industry updates. Take business or marketing courses. Get a consultation to help you improve an area of your business.

Don't go into panic mode if you're experiencing a lull – be proactive and do stuff to prevent it from happening again.

Manage your marketing

As mentioned above, inconsistent marketing greatly contributes to the feast and famine cycle. Think of it like exercise – if you stop doing it, you stop seeing results.

Be consistent

Bombarding your social media followers or email subscribers with promotional messages when you need sales and then going completely silent for weeks when you're busy is not a good strategy.

Be visible all the time, not just when you want something.

If you've used your quiet time to create social posts and content, you can continue marketing yourself when you're busy. You only need a couple of minutes a day to put a post out, or you can even pre-schedule your content.

Set realistic targets for the level of content you can put out all year round, not just at quiet times. Three social media posts a week. One blog post a month. A quarterly newsletter. Whatever is manageable for you as long as you can be consistent.

Stay focused on your ideal client

When freelancers go into panic mode during a famine phase, they often start trying to appeal to anyone and everyone, offering all kinds of products, services and packages.

This dilutes your messaging and makes your marketing feel confused.

Stay focused. Tailor your marketing to your ideal clients. Talk about the problems you solve for them.

If you stay consistent with your messaging, you'll see a more consistent flow of enquiries. And you'll see more of the right type of enquiries, so you'll spend less time dealing with people you can't help.

Track your results

Which of your marketing activities get the best results? If you don't know the answer, how do you know what to do more of?

Track your results. Look at where your enquiries are coming from. Ask people how they found you. That way, you'll know where to focus your time and effort when you are busy.

And if you get your marketing and sales processes right, you attract more of the clients you want and get paid what you're worth.

Action time: What's keeping you trapped?

Time to figure out what's holding you back.

Are you taking on the wrong kind of work?

Are you taking on too many frogs?

Are you getting distracted by bad business advice?

Are you living invoice to invoice?

Do you neglect your marketing when you're in a feast phase?

Do you panic sell when you hit a famine phase?

Take some time to think about which clients are draining your time. Can you fix the problem, or do you need to get rid of them?

Figure out what you need to change to break the feast and famine cycle – get control of your money, time, and marketing.

What's keeping you trapped?

The story so far: Part two summary

Key takeaways:

- Don't waste energy on things that don't move you closer to your goal.
- Avoid toxic clients – focus on attracting the clients you want and delivering a fantastic service.
- Not all advice is good advice – be wary of who you listen to, and don't blindly follow the pack.
- Learn from multiple sources and apply the most relevant parts to your business.
- Feast and famine is not inevitable – you can break the cycle if you get control of your money, time, and marketing.

Action points:

- Get rid of bad clients – let the relationship come to a natural end or give the required notice.
- If you're stuck in a feast or famine cycle, figure out what is keeping you trapped.

Coming up next:

- How to stop getting in the way of your own success.

Part three: Tackle your inner troll

Be more billy goat

When I was young, I had a copy of The Three Billy Goats Gruff. The story goes there were three billy goats – small, medium and large. They'd eaten all the grass on their side of the river, but on the other side, the grass was lush and green.

To get to the good grass, they had to cross the wooden bridge, but it was guarded by a troll who wanted to eat them up. The first two billy goats trick the troll into letting them pass by suggesting he wait for the next billy goat, who is bigger and more likely to satisfy his appetite.

But the biggest billy goat doesn't bother with tricks. He tackles the troll head-on, knocking him off the bridge, never to be seen again. The three billy goats get their lush green grass and live happily ever after.

You need to be like the billy goats gruff and get trolls out of your way. I'm not talking about trolls on social media – the arseholes who have nothing better to do than leave negative comments on your posts.

I'm talking about the main thing stopping you from getting to that green grass – to that happy ever after. I'm talking about you.

You are the only one stopping you from getting where you want to be – whether through procrastination, self-doubt, or resistance to change.

You don't have to charge low prices. You don't have to take on every project that comes your way. You don't have to do work you don't enjoy.

But only you can make the changes you need to get your business where you want it to be.

You will only stop getting low-paying work if you stop accepting low-paying work.

You will only stop getting shitty clients if you stop accepting shitty clients.

You will only stop being too busy if you stop overloading yourself with work.

So be more billy goat. Get that troll out of your way.

The stories we tell ourselves

There are hundreds of books and articles about fixed and growth mindset, limiting beliefs, breaking and forming habits, and how to change your thinking.

Why?

Because our thinking holds us back. We tell ourselves we can't do something and then create false stories about why we can't do that thing.

How many times have you created stories about other people?

"They won't be happy about that"

"They're going to take it really badly"

"They'll be so upset/angry/disappointed."

You build it up in your mind, only for it to be completely wrong – the person doesn't react the way you thought they would at all.

And if you can create false stories about other people, you can create false stories about yourself.

"I'm not good enough"

"I'm not experienced enough"

"People won't take me seriously"

"I'm not as confident as other people"

"I don't have enough time"

"I'm not ready yet"

Excuses. Excuses. Excuses.

The trick is to tell yourself new stories. Get those trolls out the way.

Let's take a look at some of those false stories you need to rewrite...

"I'm just a freelancer"

So what? What does "just" a freelancer even mean?

Does it mean you can't charge the same prices as an agency? No.

If what you offer is as good as a big agency, why can't you charge as much?

A client doesn't care whether you work from your back bedroom or a fancy office. They are paying for the thing you deliver, not your overheads.

Does it mean you have to accept crappy clients? No.

You're an expert with valuable skills. Clients who don't treat you that way don't deserve your help.

Being a freelancer doesn't mean you can't get brilliant clients, work to terms that suit you, or command high prices. Being a freelancer means you are free to decide how and when you work and who you work for.

I know plenty of freelancers who want to give the impression their business is bigger than just them. They are afraid they won't be taken seriously if potential clients know they are a one-person band.

Bullshit.

It's a false story we tell ourselves.

As I made clear in the first part of this book, you don't have to have a huge team to be successful.

I know plenty of people who tried hiring a team or building a team of subcontractors and then gave up because they realised it wasn't what they wanted. They didn't go into business to manage people – they went into business to do the thing they love.

And one person can often give a much better service than a whole team of people because they are the only person working on the project. There's no weak link. No passing the buck. No miscommunication.

The thing you offer your clients doesn't become any less valuable just because you're a one-person team. It doesn't become any less valuable just because you work for yourself and not a big company. And it doesn't become any less valuable if you only work part-time.

As long as you can solve a problem or make someone's life or business better, you are good enough.

"I'll never be as good as them"

"Mirror, mirror on the wall, who is fairest of them all?"

Snow White's stepmother had it all – looks, brains, magic, a castle, loyal employees, and a lovely stepdaughter.

But do you know what her downfall was? She was too concerned about how she compared to other people.

She spent too much time asking her mirror who was the fairest of all instead of cracking on with something productive.

Comparing yourself with others is not useful, especially if you're comparing yourself based on what they share on social media.

Social media only tells half the story – people put a filtered view of their life and business online, which can make others feel inadequate.

But your business is not the same as theirs.

You wouldn't walk into a gym, look at the fittest, strongest, most toned and muscular person there, and expect to achieve the same look after a single workout (unless you're deluded).

So why on earth would you compare your success to the success of others?

You aren't the same. Your clients aren't the same. Your skills and experience aren't the same. Your goals aren't the same.

You don't know what support they're getting in the background. Or whether they're exaggerating their success stories.

You don't know how long it took them to get to that point, how hard they had to work, or how much they invested.

You don't know which bits of their business they're not sharing on social media. Maybe they're in a world of debt. Maybe they are working sixteen hours a day but barely making ends meet. Perhaps they are on the verge of burning out.

I could go on, but hopefully, you get the point.

Your business is your business, and it doesn't matter what everyone else is doing or not doing.

Focus on what you're doing, which is building a business that makes you happy. And you get to decide what that looks like. Stop comparing yourself with others.

“That won’t work for me”

How do you know? Have you tried it?

And what’s the worst that can happen if you try something and it doesn’t work?

When I started charging clients upfront, I started with a 25% deposit – nobody questioned it. So, I started asking for 50% upfront. I added it to my proposals under payment terms “50% advance payment and 50% on completion of first drafts.” Again, no pushback.

Eventually, I moved to 100% upfront for new clients.

Not long after I’d started charging upfront, I landed a new client. He agreed to my price, but I hadn’t sent my standard proposal template and hadn’t told him it was advance payment.

I told myself, “I can’t charge him upfront now because I didn’t make it clear they were the terms.”

But I decided to go for it anyway. If he refused, I could make an exception this one time.

So I told him I was delighted he wanted to proceed and would send over the invoice shortly. I sent the invoice, and he paid within the hour.

The story I had told myself was wrong.

"That won't work for me" or "I can't do that" almost always translates into "I don't want to try it".

We're scared to try new things, especially if it goes against the grain. But you don't need me to tell you the human race would never have advanced if nobody had ever tried anything new.

Think of all the things we take for granted today – cars, aeroplanes, mobile phones, computers, the internet – none of which would exist if the inventors had told themselves "that won't work".

And I'm sure they had other people telling them it wouldn't work. But they ignored those people and told themselves a different story.

You're not trying to invent the internet – you're trying to create a business that makes you happy. It's not quite the same scale, so stop telling yourself, "that won't work for me", and start finding out whether it will.

Instead of asking what happens if I try and don't get the result I want, ask yourself what happens if you don't try, and things stay exactly as they are – would that make you happy?

"I'm not good enough"

Ah yes – good old imposter syndrome. It creeps up on you when you need it least, telling you what a big old fraud you are. Who on earth do you think you are, pretending you know how to do this stuff?

It's amazing how quickly you can go from thinking, "I've got this", to "I haven't got a clue what I'm doing."

It doesn't matter that you are more than capable of doing it – it's the fact you have the audacity to believe in yourself.

Imposter syndrome is just self-doubt. Sometimes it's valid – we're nervous because we've never done that thing before. Nothing wrong with being nervous – it means we care about it. But sometimes, it's completely invalid.

All too often, self-doubt is caused by fear.

Fear of being wrong.

Fear of looking stupid.

Fear of making a mistake.

Fear of getting criticism.

Fear of not getting results.

A little bit of fear and self-doubt now and again can be healthy – we should never be so arrogant as to think we're perfect and have nothing left to learn.

But if self-doubt is constantly getting in your way, you need to address it. Tell yourself a different story – change your way of thinking.

Get good enough. Invest in self-development – keep learning.

Figure out what you need to do to be good enough, then do it.

"I haven't got time"

"Just waiting until I've got my website perfect"

"Going to do a big launch after Christmas"

"I need to nail down my tone of voice before I start putting anything on social media"

"Just need to get this big client project out the way"

"As soon as my income is a bit more stable, I'm going to start investing in my business"

More excuses.

You control how you spend your time, so if you want to start today, you can.

It's easy to find an excuse to delay change or start something new. People do it all the time with diets and exercise, writing a book, or taking up a new hobby, and they do it with business development.

Why?

Maybe because it is overwhelming – we look at the goal in its entirety, and it feels too hard to get there.

Breaking big goals down into smaller goals makes them way more manageable. I didn't write this book in a day – I broke it down and worked on it in stages. A chapter at a time until it was ready.

Don't think about tomorrow – focus on what you need to do today to get closer to your goal.

"I'll never be able to do that"

Until I met my husband, I didn't exercise at all, but he's been running since he was a teenager.

Every year since 2002, he's completed the Great North Run – a half marathon (13.1 miles or around 21 kilometres).

Back in 2014, I asked if he thought I could ever do a half marathon, and he told me I absolutely could if I trained. He suggested I enter the Great North Run ballot. If I didn't get a place, it was no loss. If I did, I could decide if I wanted to attempt it.

So, I entered the ballot and got a place.

I asked him what a respectable time would be, and he said anything under two hours was really good. So that became the goal.

I had six months to train.

I worked out I needed to run all 13.1 miles at a pace of around 9 minutes per mile to get under two hours.

For my first training run, I set a target of 3 miles at a 9-minute mile pace.

What a joke that was!

My first mile was not even close to 9 minutes. And after 1.5 miles, I gave up, burst into tears, and walked home.

My two-hour goal felt impossible.

But I'm a stubborn little thing when I want to be, so I carried on training. And six months later, I crossed the line in 1 hour, 59 minutes, and 57 seconds. I achieved my goal.

It wasn't easy. Throughout the training, there were so many times I didn't think I'd be able to do it. And even on the day, there were moments I felt like just giving up. But I pushed through. And I did it.

It just shows that you can achieve your goals (however impossible they might seem) if you are willing to put in the work. But you'll never achieve those goals if you don't 'put your trainers on' and get started.

It's the same for most things in life – losing weight, writing a book, learning a skill, starting or growing a business. Set the goals, put the work in, and you'll get where you want to be.

I couldn't have woken up on day one and ran 13 miles in under two hours. But I put the work in and did what was required to get my desired result. One mile at a time.

Same with this book. I didn't wake up one day and bang out the entire thing. I did it over time – planning, writing, editing, planning, writing, editing – until it came together. One page at a time.

And I did it with my business. I set my goals and then put in the work to achieve them. One day at a time.

If you want to create your dream business, it won't happen overnight. If you are looking for overnight success or "magic beans", you'll be looking forever.

But if you start putting the work in today, you will get where you want to be.

How long it takes depends on what your happy ever after looks like and how committed you are to creating it.

You can buy the fancy kit, learn all the theories, and make grand plans, but until you put your trainers on and start running, you're never going to get to the finish line.

Are you ready to start running?

Action time: What do you need to change?

Time to be honest with yourself. Completely honest.

What is wrong with your business?

What isn't working?

I want you to make a list.

But not a list of excuses or problems. Not things like "my clients never pay on time."

I want you to make a list of things you are accountable for:

- *"I don't charge enough"*
- *"I spend too long on social media without getting results"*
- *"I compare myself with others too often"*
- *"I don't have a system for generating leads"*
- *"I don't have a clear marketing message"*
- *"I don't take payment upfront"*
- *"I agree to too many free calls"*
- *"I discount my prices"*

- *"I take on work I don't enjoy"*
- *"I never meet deadlines on time"*
- *"I take on too much work"*
- *"I answer client calls when I should ignore them"*
- *"I procrastinate too often"*
- *"I take criticism badly"*
- *"I let self-doubt hold me back"*
- *"I worry about what others think of me"*
- *"I say yes when I should really say no*
- *"I keep doing the same things even though they don't get me the right results"*

You get the picture.

What we're trying to do here is understand what is stopping you from getting to that happy ever after. Is it your pricing? Your marketing (or lack of it)? Your sales process? Your confidence? Your time management? A bit of everything?

You've got to be honest with yourself here. Only you will see your list, so there's no reason not to be.

Don't be like our emperor. Don't be too proud to admit you are getting things wrong or doing things that don't work.

The first step to change is understanding what needs to change. Then we can get to work on changing it.

What do you need to change?

The story so far: Part three summary

Key takeaways:

- The only person holding you back is yourself – stop telling yourself false stories.
- Don't compare yourself to other people – their business is not the same as your business.
- Don't be afraid of trying new things – you might be surprised by the results.
- If you don't feel good enough, figure out how to get good enough.
- You won't achieve your goals if you don't take action – set the goals, do the work.

Action points:

- Make a list of what you need to change – what's stopping you from getting where you want to be?

Coming up next:

- Building a business that works around you.

PART FOUR: BUILD YOUR HOUSE OUT OF BRICKS

Your business - your terms

Remember the three little pigs? One built a house of straw, one of sticks, and one of bricks. Along came a big bad wolf and blew down the first two, but he couldn't topple the house of bricks no matter how much he huffed and puffed.

Your business needs to be built out of bricks.

I'm not talking physical bricks and mortar. I'm talking metaphorical bricks – strict "rules" that form the structure of your business.

Rules for yourself and rules for your clients.

You set these rules to suit you. And then you stick to them no matter what.

If you don't stick to them, you might as well have built a house from straw or sticks. You'll make it easy for the big bad wolf to blow your house down.

So what rules should you set? Well, that's entirely up to you and depends on the nature of your business.

The rules you set should be in place to help you create your happy ever after.

And you have to enforce them. You don't let clients choose whether they agree to them or not – remember, we're building brick houses, not straw houses.

If a client doesn't agree to your terms or follow your processes, you don't work with them.

It sounds simple – and it is. But it's not easy to implement. It takes practice to enforce your rules.

I'm going to share some ideas for rules you can put in place and some of the rules I have in my business. If you find yourself thinking, "that won't work for me", give yourself a swift kick and try it. You might be surprised.

You decide your working hours

Rules around working hours are entirely up to you and should fit your lifestyle. If you want to take every Friday off, do it. If you prefer to work from dusk until dawn, you can. If you want to work seven days a week, that's your prerogative.

You fit your working hours to suit you.

You don't have to advertise your working hours. If you finish at 3pm because you have to do the school run, then you finish at 3pm. Clients don't need to know when you work, just that you'll get the work done.

But if you want to let clients know, then let them know – "my working hours are 9am to 3pm, Monday to Friday."

Why wouldn't they accept it? We don't question a restaurant's opening hours – if they are open from 7pm to 10pm, we just book a table between those times.

Personally, I don't have set working hours, but my working hours mainly match my husband's – I work when he works. Not always – sometimes I'll take time off in the week and catch up on an evening or weekend. Sometimes I'll work more hours because I feel like it. And sometimes I take an extra day off just because I can.

But the flexibility in my working hours is to suit me, not my clients. If a client needs work urgently and I don't have plans, I'll accommodate their needs. If I do have plans, I don't change them. Their lack of organisation isn't my problem.

Client work should not take priority over other important things – family, friends, your health (physical or mental), or business development.

People struggle with this. They put time in their calendar to work on their marketing, or go to the gym, or meet up with friends, but end up cancelling their plans to accommodate a client.

Don't.

If you want to go to the gym every Wednesday morning, then stick to it. If you want time each week to work on your marketing, block the time out and treat it like an important meeting that can't be cancelled. And if you've made plans with friends, don't cancel on them – they might really need to see you.

I have Monday mornings blocked out for planning and business development time. I schedule time to exercise at least three times a week. And if I make plans with friends, I block time out of my diary and stick to it.

Even if you are flexible with your time, make sure it's on your terms. Make "not cancelling plans with friends" one of your rules. Make "not working on holiday" one of your rules. Make "no client calls on Mondays" one of your rules.

Whatever works for you.

If you're worried about implementing these rules, don't be. For new clients, it's easy. You just tell them when you will be available or when the project will be completed.

For example, if you're a copywriter, give them a date for when they can expect their first drafts. If it's a month from now because you're on holiday for two weeks, then it's a month from now.

If they need it sooner, they either have to compromise or find someone who can accommodate them.

And what about existing clients?

Same thing. You don't have to work to their schedule. Just tell them when you will be available. And if they're used to calling you at all hours of the day, just be honest with them:

"I'm no longer answering work calls after 6pm." And then stop answering calls.

Most clients will be understanding. And any clients that aren't? Well, you need to question whether you want to work with a client who doesn't respect your time.

Don't answer unscheduled calls

This was one of the changes I made in my business. I no longer answer unscheduled calls (unless it's family or a close friend calling).

I used to answer my phone whenever it rang – I wanted clients to feel like I was accessible, and I didn't want to miss any new enquiries.

The problem with answering your phone whenever it rings is you get caught off guard. You aren't prepared for the call.

With new enquiries, it's better to schedule a planned call so you can research their company, plan your questions, and get any information you need before the call. And you can allow enough time for the call. It will feel more organised, and you'll feel more prepared.

Answering a call to a potential new client five minutes before you're due in a meeting or while you're out doing your weekly shop isn't going to be beneficial to either of you.

And the same goes for existing clients. You might think they are calling about one thing, but it turns out to be something else. Then you're on the back foot.

Plus, if you're in the middle of a project for one client when another client calls, your attention will be taken away from your work, and it'll take time to refocus.

Client A wouldn't want another client interrupting you while you're working on their project, so they can't expect you to drop what you are doing every time they call.

And that's what you need to remember. Every time you answer an unexpected call, you take time away from something else. Should demanding clients take priority over less demanding clients? Should potential clients take priority over clients who are already paying you?

Callers can leave a voicemail if it's urgent, or they can email you. You can even let clients know when you start working together that they will need to schedule calls in advance if they want to speak to you.

There are online tools available that allow clients to book time in your calendar for a call – send the link and let them pick a slot that works for them and you.

And take your phone number off your website and social media pages. Make it clear that enquiries should be via email, an enquiry form, or a booked call. You might lose a couple of impatient prospects, but if they can't wait 24 hours to speak to you, they'll probably turn out to be pretty demanding clients anyway.

Be strict with enquiries

You don't want to spend your days "jumping" on calls or meeting with prospects who will never buy. You need rules about how you deal with enquiries.

Even if you want to offer free discovery calls or briefing calls, have a process for filtering out the people you can't help or don't want to help.

I don't offer free calls. If I get an enquiry, I ask questions to find out whether I can help them (and whether I want to) and then offer a paid consultation call. If it turns out I can't help, they get their money back.

Some people don't feel comfortable with that process – no problem. If you don't want to charge, at least be selective about who you offer free calls to.

Don't just fill your days with calls and meetings on the off chance some of them will turn into work. You'll end up being busy but not making any money.

If you get an enquiry along the lines of, *"I want a chat about your services, can you call me on 0123456789"* don't rush to dial the number. Go back to them and ask if there is something specific they need help with.

Before I started doing this, I got my time wasted by numerous people wanting to "chat about my services".

Sometimes I'd arrange a time to call, and they wouldn't answer. Sometimes what they needed wasn't something I could help with. Sometimes they'd just want to pump me for free advice, then I'd never hear from them again.

My time was being wasted because I wasn't asking a couple of simple questions.

Don't get caught out. Find out whether the call is going to be worth your time before rushing in.

Charge upfront

Some of the biggest problems freelancers come across stem from not having clear terms. Terms around what you expect from clients and what they can expect from you.

You don't necessarily have to have written terms and conditions, but these can be useful.

However, one thing you should definitely have clear is your payment terms.

The easiest way to make sure you get paid is to charge upfront. Make your rule "I don't start work until I've been paid." That way, you eliminate late-paying clients or non-payers.

Trust me, charging upfront takes away a lot of headaches.

If you don't feel comfortable charging 100% upfront to begin with, insist on a deposit – this can be a set fee or a percentage of the total fee.

Even if standard practice in your industry is to charge on completion of the work, there's no reason you can't charge upfront.

Think about the hotel industry – sometimes you pay when you book, sometimes you pay at check-in, and sometimes you pay when you leave.

Same when you eat out – sometimes you order at the bar and pay, other times you get a bill at the end of your meal. You don't question it – you just accept the way that particular business chooses to operate.

And good clients will accept the way you operate. It's your business, your terms.

If a client has agreed your price, they have the budget for it. And if they have the budget for it, why can't they pay in advance?

They can.

And if you have a client who refuses to pay, then find out why they are refusing. If it's because they don't trust you, then you've got some work to do. If they can't give a reason, then you have to wonder whether they have any intention of paying.

Make yourself a priority

You cannot give your clients the best of you if you are not looking after yourself. Working yourself into the ground is not something to be proud of. Putting your clients before yourself and your family is not something to be proud of.

When you don't eat properly, when you don't sleep properly, and when you don't give yourself time to enjoy life or relax, it's not a sign that you put your customers first. It's a sign that you don't value yourself.

You might think you're doing your clients a favour by neglecting yourself to serve them, but you're not.

There is a reason they tell you on aeroplanes to put your oxygen mask on before helping others – you can't help anyone if you can't breathe. Don't kill yourself for your business.

If you want your happy ever after, you have to look after your health – physical and mental.

I think regular exercise is vital as a business owner. It's one of those things that often gets neglected but should be a priority. Exercising isn't just good for physical health – it reduces stress and anxiety.

I make exercise a priority. It's not because I enjoy it or want the physical benefits. I do it because I like how I feel after, and it benefits my mental health.

If I'm feeling overwhelmed, anxious, stressed, or the words aren't flowing, I go for a run or do a workout. Even just taking half an hour out every day to go for a walk will help you build a better business.

But if exercise isn't your thing, it's still important to take time out to do something non-work related. Read, paint, walk, cook, do a jigsaw puzzle, watch a film, go for a massage – whatever it is that helps you de-stress.

Making time to do things that aren't business-related might sound unproductive, but it actually makes you more productive. While you're taking a break, your subconscious is busy working on stuff in the background. I can't tell you how often I come back from a run brimming with ideas.

Whatever your thing is, don't feel guilty setting aside time to do it, whether it's 30 minutes a day, a couple of hours a week, or a full day a week. Make it a priority. Put it in your diary and treat it like a client meeting – something that can't be missed.

Your business isn't anybody else's business

People will have opinions on how you run your business, how you market yourself, how much you charge, what you say yes to, what you say no to. Most of those opinions will be irrelevant.

How you choose to run your business is up to you.

As long as you aren't doing anything illegal, immoral, or unethical, you can run your business how you like. Have confidence in your convictions and trust your judgement.

No matter what you do, you will never get everyone to like you or agree with you. It's not possible. And if people don't like you or agree with you, there's no point wasting your energy trying to change their opinions of you.

A lot of people go into business wanting to be liked by everyone. And so they place too much value on other people's opinions.

The best thing you can do if you want a happy business and a happy life is to stop concerning yourself with what other people think of you.

You cannot control their thoughts or feelings, but you can control how you let their thoughts and feelings affect you.

Stop wasting energy thinking about those people who'll never appreciate you.

Action time: What are your non-negotiables?

Now it's time for you to build your brick house. What are your rules? What are your non-negotiables?

Your goal is to build a business that allows you to live your happy ever after. You want clients who respect you and value what you do, not clients who treat you like shit.

Make rules that align with your goals and your values. If you don't want to work with businesses in a certain industry, make it a rule not to take on clients in that industry. If you don't want to take on projects under a certain size or value, make it a rule not to take on projects under that size or value.

And make your rules things you can control, for example:

- No answering client emails before X or after Y
- No answering unscheduled calls
- No working on holiday
- No client work on Sundays
- No free discovery calls
- Don't work with unethical businesses

- Online meetings only unless they pay for travel
- Only deal with decision-makers
- Minimum project rate is £X
- Minimum contract term is X months
- Only one set of amends per project
- Get paid upfront
- Charge for discovery calls

These are all things that you have control over. If you say, "no calls after 6pm", you can just stop answering your phone after 6pm.

Things like "I will make £X per month" are targets – you cannot control them. We'll be setting some targets later, but for now, we're setting rules.

Don't make rules you know you won't stick to. These have got to be things you are prepared to do, even if they make you feel a little uncomfortable at first.

You can start by implementing rules for new clients first – for example, "from today, all new clients have to pay upfront". Then once you are comfortable with your new ways of working, apply your rules to existing clients.

Most of your clients won't mind you setting boundaries – I certainly wouldn't have a problem with a supplier letting me know they now only reply to emails between 10am and 3pm.

And any clients that do make a fuss – well, you can decide whether you want to continue working with them or whether you want to focus on getting clients who are easier to deal with.

So what are your rules?

Write down at least three rules you will implement starting today. You can always add to them later, but let's make some immediate changes so we can get you closer to your happy ever after.

What are your non-negotiable rules?

The story so far: Part four summary

Key takeaways:

- You decide your working hours, not your clients.
- Put processes in place for dealing with enquiries so you don't end up on calls with timewasters.
- Charging upfront eliminates the problem of late-payers and non-payers.
- You need to look after your physical and mental health and make yourself a priority.
- Your business is nobody else's business – it's up to you how you run it.

Action points:

- Set your non-negotiable rules. Choose three that you will implement immediately.

Coming up next:

- Pricing your services based on the value you deliver.

PART FIVE: THE PRICING PARADOX

What are you worth?

I love the phrase "price is what you charge, value is what you deliver" because it sums up the way we should appraoch our fees. All too often we focus on the numerical figure we allocate to our services rather than on what that service is worth to the client, and it should be the other way around.

When I started freelancing, my pricing was based on complete guesswork. I didn't even know what other copywriters charged to know whether I was cheap, expensive, or somewhere in between.

My typical approach to pricing was, "that'll take me about X hours, so at £X per hour, that's about £X – oh wait, that sounds expensive, so I'll knock a few quid off."

Crazy!

But I suspect (actually, I know) that a lot of other freelancers work in a similar way. Because when it comes to false stories, there are plenty we tell ourselves about money and pricing.

"I can't charge that much"

"I'm not worth that much"

"Nobody will pay that"

"I want to be affordable"

"My clients wouldn't be prepared to pay that much"

"I don't want to be greedy"

That last one is common. Our fear of being perceived as greedy often stops us from charging what we are worth. We don't want to be greedy – it doesn't align with our values.

But it's not greedy to want enough money to live a happy, comfortable life.

If you earn enough to be happy, you're in a better position to help other people. If you're barely making ends meet, you will be distracted by your financial stress and anxiety.

You are not being greedy by wanting to get paid for your time, knowledge, skills, and experience. Those things are valuable, even if you are just starting your freelance career.

And if you genuinely sell something of value, it's not unreasonable to sell it for what it is worth.

Price is what you charge

Don't base your pricing on what you need to earn to cover your costs. Other people will be offering the same services, but they'll be charging more because their costs are higher. And just because you don't need as much money as them doesn't mean you shouldn't charge the same.

If you were employed and your employer offered everyone doing your role a pay rise, you wouldn't turn it down just because your mortgage payments were lower than your colleague's. You'd be doing the same amount of work, so you'd expect to get the same reward. Why should it be different when you work for yourself?

Your overheads – business or personal – are not relevant to what you charge. The only relevant thing is the value you add and the quality of service you deliver.

Price is just a number.

This porridge is too hot!

Remember the story of Goldilocks? She was a picky little thing. "This porridge is too hot. This porridge is too sweet."

People are like that with pricing too.

You might think keeping your prices low will make you appeal to a wider audience – it won't.

Some people see "cheap" and automatically think "crap". Most people understand that quality comes at a cost. If your prices are too low, you'll put some people off.

Equally, high prices aren't for everyone. You will always get price-driven buyers. They'll look for a lower-cost option no matter how good of a job you do at justifying your prices.

Focus on clients who are more interested in the result you deliver rather than the cost.

Hourly pricing is flawed

Hourly pricing is one of the easiest ways to price, which is why so many freelancers, coaches, and consultants offer an hourly rate or day rate for their services.

But hourly pricing is flawed. Your clients aren't paying for your time – they are paying for your knowledge, skills, and experience.

Let's say you're a VA, and you charge the standard rate for VAs. What happens if you're faster at certain tasks than other VAs? You deliver the same outcome, but you're faster, so you earn less? That doesn't make much sense.

Why should you be paid less than your counterparts simply because you are faster?

Plus, working at an hourly rate means you only get paid for billable hours. What about all the time spent on tasks like marketing and admin? What about any costs for licenses, software, or tools needed to deliver your work? Does your hourly pricing account for all these things?

Even if it does, it means you probably have to work a set number of billable hours each week – what happens if you have a slow month? Or you're on holiday for a week?

The nature of freelancing means it can be very unpredictable. You can tell yourself you need to complete 30 hours of billable work per week, but that doesn't mean you're going to have enough work to fill 30 hours.

And that leads to a situation where you have to take on extra work in future weeks, which then takes time away from other things – usually marketing.

Then because you aren't doing any marketing, you have no work lined up for when your busy period ends, and you get caught in a feast and famine cycle.

Undercharging is detrimental to your clients

A common theme among freelancers is wanting to be affordable. But affordable is subjective, and freelancers often end up being underpriced instead.

And when you are underpriced, you usually end up overworked. Firstly, because most people will agree to your low prices, so you get a lot of clients. And secondly, because you have to take on a high volume of work to hit your financial targets.

This isn't only unfair to you. It's unfair to your clients too.

Let's say you charge £500 per project and you need to earn £2000 a week to cover all your costs. This means you need four projects a week. You have to divide your attention between four clients.

But if you charge £1000 a project, you only need two clients, and you can give those two clients double your time.

How much better is the quality of your service going to be if you only have to split your attention between two projects instead of four?

Now let's say you charge £2000 a project. Now you only have one client to give all your attention to. How much better is the quality of work going to be compared to when you were splitting your time between four clients?

And you probably won't need to give that one client all the time you would have given to four clients, so you free up time for your own development.

Time you can use to read up on the latest updates in your industry. Time to complete training or invest in your learning. Time to research any new tools and software that could help you deliver an even better service.

And because you are investing time in these things, you'll be able to deliver even more value to your clients.

But if you fill your time with low-paying work, you don't have time to invest in yourself, and you do your clients a disservice.

You might think you are doing your clients a favour by keeping your pricing "affordable", but you aren't. You're not giving them the best of yourself.

You can help more people if you charge more

It's easy to fall into the trap of thinking you can help more people if you keep your prices "affordable".

But it's not always the case.

If your prices are low, you have to fill your time with client work. But if you charge decent rates, you have more time to work on free or low-cost resources.

Those free or low-cost resources can help people who cannot afford your services.

Take this book as an example – I would never have had time to write it if I was filling all my days and evenings with low-paying client work.

But because I charge a reasonable rate, I have enough flexibility to work on projects like this. And that means I can reach more people.

I can create low-cost products like books and online courses, making it easier for people with low budgets to access my support.

You could do the same.

If you charge higher prices, you don't need to fill as much of your time with billable work, so you have more time to help people who may not be able to afford your services. You could create free or low-cost resources. You could even volunteer your time and skills to a charity if you wanted.

If you are serious about helping as many people as possible, charging low prices is not the way to go about it.

So what prices should you be charging?

Unfortunately, I can't give you a number. It's up to you to determine the answer.

If you're unsure whether you can increase your prices, try it anyway. Start by applying a 20% increase to any new clients and see if it affects your conversions. If it doesn't, you can go up again.

And your existing clients? Well, that's up to you. Put their price up gradually and with notice – if they value what you do, they'll be happy to pay a little extra.

Price increases aren't unusual – they happen across every sector, so why wouldn't freelancers increase their prices too?

And if you do get some resistance, see it as an opportunity to drop some of those low-paying clients so you can focus on attracting clients who are prepared to pay what you are worth.

Value is what you deliver

How much are you worth? How do you place a value on your skills, knowledge and experience?

Most of the time, there is no right or wrong answer to how much something is worth. Buyers decide what they are prepared to pay.

A £5 handbag does the same job as a £5000 handbag, but you get buyers at either end of the scale.

Any car will get you from A to B, but some people drive around in an old banger while others splash out on top-of-the-range sports cars.

And when it comes to art? Why is one painting worthless and another priceless?

Price is just a number – it doesn't matter. What matters is the value (or perceived value) of what you deliver.

If you sell something for £1000, but that thing means your client makes an extra £100,000, they'll think they got a bargain.

And what about this book? If it gives you the confidence to double your prices (and your income), it'll pay for itself a thousand times over.

But the return on investment can't always be measured in financial return. That's where perceived value comes in.

How much is increased confidence worth? How much is happiness worth? How much is reduced stress and being able to sleep at night worth?

Well, that depends on who is buying. And that's why you need to know who your ideal clients are.

When it comes to your pricing, there will almost always be a cheaper option or a more expensive option. You need to decide which end you want to sit closer to. Then tailor your marketing to the people who think you're worth it.

That doesn't mean you pick a price and then decide who can afford you. People with tons of cash can be complete cheapskates. While people with a modest income might be prepared to pay top dollar if they really want what you've got.

We all have different priorities when it comes to money. We scrimp in some areas so we can splurge in others. Some people buy clothes from charity shops so they can afford the latest iPhone when it comes out. Some people never eat out so they have money for a luxury holiday every year.

Never make assumptions about what your ideal client can afford – they might have a low turnover business, but they might also be mortgage-free with a load of savings in the bank. If you can convince them you have something of value, they'll have no problem finding the cash.

The most important thing to remember

Your fees should reflect the quality of your service. If you knowingly don't deliver value for money, you should take a long, hard look at yourself.

But if you genuinely offer something of value, there's no reason not to charge accordingly.

You can put any price you want on your services. You can be the lowest priced in your field or the highest. But price is just a number. It's not cash in the bank.

It will only be cash in the bank if you can get people to pay it. And you can only do that if your marketing attracts the right people and you know how to convert them into clients.

That means you've got to be able to create the right messages and get them in front of the right people. It means you have to demonstrate you can deliver on your promises and that delivering on those promises will be worth the investment.

That's the hard part.

Action time: Are your prices too low?

Here's an easy test to find out whether your prices are too low:

Write down how many hours you work on average each week, including marketing, admin, client work, meetings, calls – everything business related. Now write down how many hours you'd ideally like to work in your happy ever after.

Next, write down your average monthly income and your ideal average monthly income.

If the hours you work are higher than you'd like and your income is lower than you'd like, then your pricing is wrong. And if you ever want your happy ever after, you need those prices to go up.

Increase your prices from today, starting with any new clients. If you work on fixed pricing, add 20% (don't forget to update any price lists). If you quote on a project-by-project basis, add 20% to what you usually charge.

If your conversion rates don't drop significantly, you can probably increase your prices even more.

Are your prices too low?

The story so far: Part five summary

Key takeaways:

- Price is what you charge. Value is what you deliver. Focus on value.
- If you genuinely offer something of value, then it's not greedy to charge for it.
- Pricing too low is detrimental to your clients – you can deliver a better service if you charge more.
- Hourly pricing is flawed – people are paying for your knowledge, skills, and experience, not your time.
- If you work more hours than you'd like but earn less than you'd like, your prices are too low.

Action points:

- If you're prices are too low, increase them by 20%. If your conversion rates don't drastically drop, increase them a little more.

Coming up next:

- Who is your ideal client, and why does it matter?

PART SIX: THE RIGHT PEOPLE

Who do you want to attract?

Marketing is not as complicated as you might think.

In fact, it's really quite simple: You've got to get the right message in front of the right people at the right time.

The reason so many people fail to attract good clients usually comes down to one or more of the following:

They don't identify the right people – they don't know who their ideal clients are.

They don't get their messaging right – they focus on what they do, not the problems they solve.

They don't use the right channels, platforms, or tactics to get in front of their ideal clients.

In this part of the book, we're going to look at "the right people" – who are your ideal clients?

If you don't know who you want to work with, it will be much harder to attract them.

To niche or not to niche

When I was a newbie copywriter, I didn't specialise in a specific industry. I wrote for any type of business. I liked the variety – loved learning about new things all the time.

I started out by offering various copywriting services – websites, blogs, direct mail, brochures, emails and so on. I created all kinds of packages so people could pick one that worked for them.

Then I realised not everyone could afford a copywriter, so I started running training workshops.

Then someone asked me to train their team, so I added team training to my service offering. And then I added more and more services so I could appeal to more and more people.

Then one day, the penny dropped. My marketing wasn't attracting the right people because my messaging was too confusing.

By trying to appeal to everyone, I wasn't making it clear who I helped. And by giving people too many options to choose from, I was leaving them overwhelmed with decisions.

Suddenly I understood why so many marketers and business coaches were banging on about having a niche.

A niche doesn't limit you – it focuses you. And it makes it so much easier to attract the clients and the work you want.

You might be worried you'll miss out on work if you focus your marketing messages too much. But you'll miss out on more of the work you want if you don't focus your marketing messages at all.

Think about it this way: if you had a problem with your heart, who would you trust more to fix it – a general surgeon or a specialist heart surgeon?

What if you had just spent a fortune on a new car and it broke down? Would you rather take it to a generalist garage or hire a mechanic who specialises in that make of car?

If a builder is looking for an accountant, do you think they'd be more likely to choose a generalist accountant or someone specialising in accounting for construction businesses?

And if someone is looking for a copywriter to write a direct mail letter, do you think they would prefer a generalist copywriter or someone specialising in direct mail?

If you were recruiting, you'd sift through CVs and invite the candidates with the most relevant skills and experience to interview.

When your clients are looking for someone to help them, they are doing a similar thing – choosing the person with the most relevant skills and experience. Make sure that's you.

Niching down

You can niche in different ways:

By the clients you serve. For example, you can focus on clients in a specific industry, sector, or location, work with businesses of a certain size, turnover, or age, or work with individuals in a specific demographic.

By the products and services you offer. For example, a copywriter could specialise in email marketing, video scripts, landing pages, or Facebook ads.

By the problem you solve. For example, a therapist might specialise in easing back pain caused by chronic sciatica.

But the more specific you can be about what you offer or who you offer it to, the easier it will be to get your marketing messages clear.

You don't want to attract a load of clients you don't like or spend your days working on projects you don't enjoy. And if you get your marketing messages right, you don't have to. You can attract the work you want at the prices you want to charge.

My ideal clients are freelancers, coaches, consultants, or service providers who are good at what they do but aren't getting the clients they want.

And so I tailor all my marketing to people who fit that description. This book is written for them.

But that doesn't mean I don't work with people who aren't an exact match for my ideal client profile.

Tailoring your marketing to your ideal client doesn't mean you can never work with people who don't fit the bill or never take on projects that don't meet all your criteria.

It just means you attract more of the clients and work you do want, so you can be more selective about what else you say yes to.

Your ideal client isn't "anyone"

Your ideal clients cannot be "anyone". There are always parameters, so start with the most obvious details about your ideal clients.

Are they business owners, employees, job seekers, students, or retirees? Is location important?

If you work with businesses, does the size or age of a business matter – do you want to work with start-ups, one-person businesses, businesses with between ten and fifty employees, or businesses with multiple sites? Do you only work with businesses or organisations in a specific sector?

If you work with individuals, does gender, age or employment status matter? Do they have to be homeowners? Do they have a specific hobby or interest? Is income a factor?

I know I said you can't make assumptions about what your ideal client will consider affordable, but there will be some limitations. For example, if you sell super yachts, you're going to be targeting the very wealthy.

The point is, whether you work with businesses or individuals, there will be some criteria your ideal clients have to meet.

Who do you want to work with?

Once you have the key attributes, it's time to narrow things down further. The more detailed you can be about your ideal client profile, the easier it will be to tailor your marketing.

I know this can be difficult if you are in the position I was in, where you have a wide variety of clients, but trust me, narrowing it down will pay off.

Picture your favourite client – the person you look forward to working with most. Or think about the project you enjoyed working on most.

Use that person or that project as a guide for working out who you would most like to work with or the type of work you would most like to attract.

Who don't you want to work with?

If you are still struggling to create a clear picture of your ideal client, think about who you don't want to work with.

You probably don't want to attract people who are focused on price – they will never see the value in what you do. They'll just be looking for the cheapest option.

You'll also want to avoid people who aren't prepared to accept your rules. People who think you should drop everything whenever they want to talk to you. People who will demand your attention when they need something and then go completely silent when you need something from them.

You might want to avoid certain types of business – I don't mentor anyone working in an MLM company because they don't have full control over their business model. And I wouldn't work with someone selling psychic services as I don't believe in that type of thing.

You might also have very strict rules regarding beliefs or values. I won't work with people who discrimninate based on gender, race, or sexuality.

I'm sure if you think about it for more than ten seconds, you'll quickly see that even if "anybody" could be your client, you don't want them to be.

Good marketing is as much about repelling the wrong people as attracting the right people.

Action time: Who are your ideal clients?

In the next part of this book, we will be looking at marketing and sales processes. You will have much greater success with this if you understand exactly who you want to work with.

Write down as many details about your ideal client as you can. Start with the obvious things like whether they are business owners, employed, self-employed, etc. And then drill down into some of the specifics – what kind of person are they?

You might serve multiple different clients at the minute but focus on the ones you want more of.

Which clients do you enjoy working with most? Which projects get you most excited?

We're trying to create your happy ever after – that means working with people because you **want** to help them, not just because you **can** help them.

So who do you want to work with?

Who are your ideal clients?

The story so far: Part six summary

Key takeaways:

- You'll have more success with your marketing if you know who you want to attract.
- The more specific you are about who you help or what you offer, the easier it is to create effective marketing messages.
- Your ideal client is not "anybody" – there will be some people you don't want to work with or can't help.
- You want your marketing to repel the wrong type of people and attract the right kind of people.
- Don't think about who you **can** help – focus on who you **want** to help.

Action points:

- Write down as many details as you can about your ideal clients.

Coming up next:

- Understanding basic marketing and sales processes.

Part seven: The right message

Get comfortable selling

Now we know who the right people are, we need to create the right message, and that's what we'll be focusing on in this part of the book.

How can you convince your ideal clients to invest in you?

I hear too many freelancers saying they don't like selling. If you don't like selling, you should reconsider your decision to work for yourself because sales is the most important part of any business.

It doesn't matter how good your products or services are if nobody is buying them. You could be the best in your field, but it doesn't matter if you don't have any customers.

If you want a business that earns you money, you've got to sell. And if you genuinely offer something of value, selling shouldn't be a problem.

I love selling.

Why?

Because I know what I sell will improve my clients' businesses. I know it will help them attract and convert more of the clients they want.

So when I sell something, it means somebody's life is about to get better. And I think that's pretty exciting.

It's not true that people don't like being sold to

Have you ever seen something in a shop window, then gone in to buy it?

Or bought something that was on special offer?

Or had someone to your house to quote for some work?

Or visited a showroom?

Or clicked on an ad?

In other words, have you ever been sold to?

Of course you have.

I sold you this book. Maybe you saw an ad for it, received an email about it, or saw me posting about it on social media. But something made you click through to the payment page and hand over your money.

And did you hate it?

Was the whole experience horrible?

If it was, I doubt you'd have made the purchase.

It's a lie that people don't like being sold to. It's just another fake story people tell themselves so they can get out of selling.

Think about it. We all like buying things. And if we like buying things, why wouldn't we like people selling to us?

We just don't like being sold to in the wrong way.

We don't like being interrupted with generic sales pitches from strangers.

We don't like being pressured into making on-the-spot decisions if we aren't sure what we're agreeing to is the right fit.

We don't like to be tricked or scammed into handing over cash for something that's shit.

And that's not how sales should be done.

Sales without the sleaze

Sales should be about offering something of value and ensuring the people who will benefit most from it know about it.

It should be about understanding the needs of your ideal clients and showing them they can trust you to solve their problems.

And that's where good marketing comes in.

You might be wondering why I'm talking about marketing in a section about selling, but it's because the two go hand in hand. The whole point of marketing is to generate leads so you can sell to them.

And that's what too many freelancers forget. They think marketing, especially content marketing, is an alternative to selling. It's not. It's just part of the process.

Someone once told me, "you either sell and then build a relationship or you build a relationship and then sell."

I think that sums things up quite well. And which option you choose depends on what you sell.

But either way, you have to sell.

There's no point building a community, a following, or a subscriber list if none of it ever turns into sales.

You can build fantastic relationships with as many "potential clients" as you want, but if they aren't paying you, they aren't clients – they are prospects.

That might sound harsh, but it's true. And it's a differentiation that's important to make.

Because if you spend your time building a brand instead of building a business, you aren't going to get your happy ever after.

So whatever marketing methods you decide to invest your time or money into, never lose sight of the end goal – turning ideal prospects into ideal clients.

And if you can genuinely help them – if you can improve their life or solve their problems – they'll be happy to pay for your support.

Sales funnels and stepping stones

Some companies have completely separate marketing and sales departments, but for most small businesses, the line is blurred. At what point in the process do you stop marketing and start selling?

It shouldn't be obvious – certainly not to your prospects. It should feel like a natural progression.

You've probably heard the term marketing funnel or sales funnel. I hate the term funnel – I think it's so impersonal. I prefer to call it a process. But whether you call it a process, a funnel, or something else, it essentially works in the same way.

You need to **attract** the right people and then **nurture** them until they are ready to **convert** into paying clients.

The attract stage is about attracting attention and getting your message in front of prospects. Nurturing is about building interest and desire around what you do and establishing trust and credibility. And the convert stage is getting people to take action.

Some prospects will go from the attract stage – from not having a clue who you are – to the convert stage – handing over their cash – in a matter of minutes.

But sometimes, it takes longer to get people through your sales process. And that's where your funnels come in.

You've no doubt seen a funnel in action. You download a free guide and then receive a series of emails trying to sell you something or get you to book a call.

Or you sign up for a free trial or free version of something and then receive marketing communications trying to convince you to upgrade.

The point of a funnel is to move prospects through the marketing and sales process by getting them interested in what you offer, making them want it, and building trust and credibility.

Think of it like a huge river. You have your ideal clients on one side of the river and your products or services on the other. Your goal is to get as many ideal clients as possible across the river. So you create stepping stones for them.

The more stepping stones (funnels) you create, the more chance you have of getting your ideal clients across.

Approach or attract

The first step in our marketing process is attracting the attention of our ideal clients.

There are two ways to do this:

1. Find your ideal clients and **approach** them directly
2. **Attract** your ideal clients to you

You might hear this referred to as direct and indirect marketing, push and pull marketing, or outbound and inbound marketing.

Whatever terms you use, the objective is the same – get your message in front of the right people.

The key to both is knowing who your ideal clients are.

Direct marketing

If you've ever watched The Little Mermaid (the Disney version), you'll probably remember the sea witch, Ursula.

She was brilliant at direct marketing. She figured out who her 'ideal client' was, identified their unique challenges, then approached them with the perfect solution.

In the case of our little mermaid, our crafty sea witch did her research. She realised Ariel was in love with a human and would need to become human to win him over.

So Ursula approached Ariel, showed that she understood her pain, then offered the solution. And Ariel signed the contract.

This is direct marketing. And it is exactly what it sounds like – you work out who needs what you offer and approach them directly.

If you know exactly who you want to do business with and how to get in touch with them, direct marketing can get you results much faster.

Examples of direct marketing:

- Cold calling
- Direct messaging
- Cold emails
- Direct mail
- Facebook ads
- TV, radio or press ads
- Leaflet drops

Direct marketing aims to get your message in front of people who are likely to buy.

Indirect marketing

Indirect marketing is about attracting clients to you.

Think about the witch in the story of Hansel and Gretel. She knows exactly who she wants to attract – tasty children. So she creates something she knows will appeal to them – a gingerbread house. Once she has their attention, she moves them to the next step of her process – she lures them inside.

I'll admit, her intentions were pretty grim, but the point is she knew how to attract her 'ideal clients' to her.

And this is the premise of indirect marketing, particularly content marketing. You create content that appeals to your ideal audience, and then once you have their attention, you move them to the next stage.

This sounds like a nicer, softer approach than direct marketing, but it doesn't require any less effort. In fact, it can be much harder than direct marketing and more time-consuming.

You can't guarantee your message will get in front of the right people, and it can be difficult to track the return on investment.

Examples of indirect marketing:

- Content marketing
- PR
- Social media
- Influencer marketing
- Sponsorship
- Search engine optimisation (SEO)
- Refer a friend schemes

The great thing about direct and indirect marketing is you don't have to pick one or the other. You can do both.

And both methods can be highly effective when done well. But both can be a huge waste of time and effort when done badly.

We'll look at different marketing methods in more detail later, but first, let's look at what you need to do once you have the attention of your ideal prospects.

Interest, desire, trust, and credibility

Once you've got the attention of your ideal prospects, you need to turn them into clients.

Do they need what you offer? If not, you need to generate interest.

Do they want what you offer? If not, you need to create desire.

Do they have confidence in your ability to deliver? If not, you need to build trust and establish your credibility.

Generating interest

Sometimes your ideal client will already know they need what you offer. Other times you'll need to show them they have a need.

Take cat food versus cat toys as an example.

People know they have to feed a cat – it's a given. So if you sell cat food, you don't have to convince your prospects they need cat food because they already know.

What you need to do is convince them they need **your** cat food. Generate interest in what you offer – what makes it better than your competitor's food? Is it cheaper, higher quality, or more nutritional?

In comparison, cat toys are not essential, so you have to create the need. You have to show people they have a problem or potential problem you can solve.

You need to generate interest in the product itself, not just your version of it. Show the benefits of the cat toys. Do they help cat owners bond with their pet? Will they stop the cat from scratching at furniture? Will they stimulate the cat and improve reflexes?

In other words, if there is already a need for what you offer, focus on selling the benefits of getting it from you. If there isn't a need already, generate interest in what you offer.

How do you do that?

Talk about the problems before you talk about the solution. Establish the need first.

Instead of: *"Our pet toys will entertain your cat for hours"*

Focus on the problem: *"Is your cat always scratching at your furniture?"*

Or identify a need they didn't know they had: *"Did you know cat toys can improve your cat's health?"*

Don't assume people know they have a problem or know what is causing the problem.

For example, compare these two pieces of copy:

My book has been created for freelancers who want to attract better clients. It'll help you improve your marketing messages and understand how to appeal to your ideal clients.

In this first example, I'm expecting readers to make a leap and connect the dots. I'm assuming they know they have a problem – bad clients – and that they know the cause of the problem – not attracting good ones.

And while you might think it's obvious that having bad clients is a result of not attracting good ones, it's not. Sometimes we are too close to a problem to see it as a problem.

Maybe our freelancers have spent too long in their echo chambers and think bad clients are just something you have to put up with.

And if they don't know they have a problem, they won't know they need to fix it, so my message won't have any impact on them. I need to show them they have a problem before I offer the solution.

Are you attracting bad clients? Clients who expect you to drop everything when they need your attention. Clients who always haggle you down on price. Clients who never pay on time. Clients who make you miserable. It doesn't have to be that way...

This example focuses on specific situations my ideal clients can relate to. And if they can relate to those situations – if they are experiencing those problems – they will be more interested in what I have to say next.

Creating desire

Interest is about showing your ideal prospects you have something they need. But desire is about making them want it.

You might think needing something automatically translates to wanting it, but it doesn't.

Think about car insurance. You need it if you have a car, but you don't necessarily want it – there are other things you'd rather spend your money on.

And just because you need something doesn't mean you need it urgently. Maybe your laptop is running slowly – you need a new one but not so urgently that you want to buy one today.

So once you have established the need and got your potential clients interested in what you offer, you have to make them want it – you have to create desire and urgency.

There are a couple of ways you can do this.

You can show them how the problem could worsen if they don't do anything about it.

Or you could show them how much better their life would be if this problem no longer existed.

Or you could give them a reason to make a decision sooner rather than later.

Exclusivity, FOMO (fear of missing out), and limited availability all drive people to buy.

But don't lie. Don't tell people it's a one-time deal or a limited offer if it's not.

I wouldn't pretend there were limited copies of this book – most people would know it was bullshit.

But I can say there is limited availability to work with me one-on-one because it's true.

There is only one of me, and there are only 24 hours a day, so I can't mentor an unlimited number of people. That's why I only take on three new mentor clients per month.

So think about how you can get your potential clients from just needing what you offer to needing it **and** wanting it.

Building trust

You might have heard it said that people are more likely to buy from you if they know, like, and trust you.

Of the three, trust is the one that matters most. It helps if people know and like you, but trust is most important.

Let's face it, you probably know some people you like but wouldn't trust with your business.

Just because someone is nice or fun to be around doesn't make them reliable or competent.

I know lots of people who I'd happily go for a drink with but wouldn't do business with.

And equally, we've probably all done business with people or companies we don't know because we trust them to deliver.

I don't know Jeff Bezos personally, and I don't know enough about him to know whether he's likeable. But I buy things from Amazon because I know if I order something, it'll turn up – I trust them to deliver.

So while it can be useful to give potential clients an insight into you and your personality so they like you, it's more important to build trust.

You can do this by demonstrating confidence in your service – money-back guarantees are a great way of doing this.

I charge for my consultation calls, but I make it clear I'll refund the fee if it turns out I can't help.

Another great way of building trust is demonstrating your expertise. Don't just tell people you're an expert – prove it.

This doesn't mean giving away your skills for free. But you can create content – blog posts, videos, social media posts, emails – showing you're an expert in your industry.

Getting published in an industry magazine or writing a book can also help you build trust and credibility.

Establishing credibility

Trust and credibility almost always go hand in hand. People are more likely to trust you if you can prove you are credible.

And one of the most effective ways of proving your credibility is getting other people to do it for you.

Feedback, reviews, case studies, and recommendations all show you are credible and can be trusted to deliver.

Ask your past clients to provide feedback and use it in your marketing.

You can tell people how brilliant you are, but they are more likely to believe it if they hear it from someone else.

Your marketing isn't about you

Marketing is about attracting clients to you, but it isn't about you. It's about your ideal clients.

Before you do anything, ask yourself:

Will this get my ideal clients interested in what I offer?

Will this create a desire to buy from/work with me?

Will this encourage my ideal clients to trust me?

Will this demonstrate my credibility?

If the answer isn't 'yes' to at least one of those questions, you need to consider why you are doing what you are doing.

And remember, the goal of your marketing is to move your ideal clients closer to the buying stage. So think about what you want them to do next.

Inspiring action

Once you've attracted your ideal prospects, got them interested in what you offer, and gained their trust, you want them to take action.

The action doesn't necessarily have to be a sale – it depends where they are in your marketing process.

The action could be to sign-up to your email list, click through to your website, or book a discovery call. Then you can continue to nurture them until they are ready to move to the next stage. Nurture, convert, nurture, convert – stepping stones.

How many times your prospects go through the nurture, convert, nurture, convert cycle and how long it takes to get people to part with their money will depend on several factors.

Some people make buying decisions quickly. They might see one of your posts on social media, click through to your website, and then book a call.

Other people are more cautious. I've had people who have been following me on social media for years or receiving my marketing emails for months before getting in touch about my services.

People will move through your marketing process at a pace that suits them.

And some people might never turn into buyers. That's ok – you don't want everyone to buy, just your ideal clients.

Low-cost, low-risk commitments

Be realistic about what action you can expect at each stage of your process.

It's unlikely someone will go from never having heard of you to signing up for a £10k training programme after seeing a single social media post.

That's not to say it can't be done, but it would be the exception, not the norm.

In most cases, it's easier to get your ideal clients to take baby steps. Start with low-risk or low-cost commitments and gradually build up to the big-ticket items.

While someone probably won't sign up for a £10k training programme off the back of a social media post, they might be prepared to request a brochure or sign up for a free guide in return for their email address.

The next commitment might be a low-cost product – a book, webinar, or event.

The goal is to take people through the process at a pace they are comfortable with.

That's what I'm doing with this book.

It's a low-cost product, so it's low-risk. I'm not asking you for a big investment, so if you read it and think it's shit, you've lost a few quid (which I'll happily refund if you ask) and a couple of hours of your time.

Because it's low-risk, it's not a difficult sell. As long as I make it clear who the book is for and how it will help them, it should attract the right people.

Most people who buy this book fit broadly with my ideal client criteria – freelancers who value happiness.

Of those buyers, some will read this book and dismiss it. Maybe they don't like me, or they don't like my style, or they don't like what I have to say. I'm not everyone's cup of tea – I'm not trying to be.

But some people will read this book, enjoy it, and want to implement what they've learnt. I hope you are one of those people.

And if you are, you might choose to do it by yourself, or you might want more of my support.

You already know me through reading this book, you know my approach and you (hopefully) know you can trust me to deliver.

So maybe you'll sign-up for some of my other services – maybe you already have.

And you might stop there, or you might go on to invest in more of my services. You might even decide you want me to mentor you one-on-one.

The point is it's a process, and you'll move through it at your own pace. Just as your ideal clients will move through your marketing process at their own pace.

Tell people what you want them to do next

Don't leave people guessing what you want them to do next. Tell them.

If you put out marketing messages or content with no call to action, you're putting the responsibility on your readers to make a decision.

Should they call you? Email you? Hunt your website for a contact form? Search for your Facebook page?

People like getting clear instructions as it makes life easier – they don't have to figure it out themselves and are less likely to make the wrong choice.

So tell people what to do next.

Make your call to action assertive. Put a verb at the beginning – an action word.

Instead of: *"If you like my content, subscribe to my newsletter"*

Say: *"Subscribe to my newsletter for more great content"*

And make taking action easy.

If you want people to click through to your website, share a link to your website. If you want them to book a call, give them a link to book. If you want them to buy something, create a payment page.

Action time: What problems do you solve?

In some ways, selling a physical product over a service is easier because you are selling something tangible – something the buyer can hold, touch, or use.

But selling a service isn't as tough as people think. Most freelancers, coaches, consultants, and service providers struggle with it because they focus on the service, not the problems it solves.

Don't think about what you do for your clients – the thing you offer. Think about how the thing you do improves their life or business.

What problems might they be experiencing right now?

You might sell website copy, but that's not what your ideal clients are buying. They are buying a solution to a problem – you need to figure out what that specific problem is.

Are they getting lots of website traffic but no enquiries?

Are they getting the wrong kind of enquiries?

Figure out what problems or challenges keep your potential clients awake at night.

What doubts, fears, and concerns are at the back of their mind?

What false stories are they telling themselves?

What are their motivations for buying?

Do they want to save time? Save money? Win more business? Stay compliant? Feel more successful? Have more confidence? Look better? Earn more? Would they be motivated by greed, fear, or vanity? Do they want to improve their health, their wealth, a relationship, a hobby, or their status?

Get in the mind of your ideal clients – what situation are they in right now that you can help them get out of, fix or improve?

Think about past clients – what reasons did they give for wanting your help, and why did they choose you over the competition? Past or current client feedback can be great for honing your marketing messages.

Ideally, you want potential clients to feel completely confident you're the right person for the job before they even speak to you. You don't want to enter into bidding wars with competitors or have to pitch to people to win their trust.

You want to already have their trust by the time they contact you. You want them to feel like you understand them – that you know what problems they have and can deliver the solution.

You can only achieve all that if you know who your ideal clients are and how you can help them.

What problems do you solve?

The story so far: Part seven summary

Key takeaways:

- You have to get comfortable with selling – if nobody buys from you, you won't last long in business.
- Create marketing processes that attract, nurture, and convert your ideal clients.
- Get clients interested in what you do, make them desire it, earn their trust, and demonstrate your credibility.
- Make your marketing messages about your clients – what problems do you solve?
- Tell people what you want them to do next – move people to the next stage of your marketing and sales process.

Action points:

- Write down all the problems or challenges that keep your ideal clients awake at night.

Coming up next:

- Choosing the right marketing channels.

PART EIGHT: THE RIGHT TIME (AND PLACE)

Be where your ideal clients are

You know who you want to attract – your ideal clients. And you know how to create the right message – focus on their problems.

Now all we need to do is get your message in the right place at the right time.

Unfortunately, we don't always know when the "right time" is. We don't always know when our clients will be in the mood to buy.

So it's easier if we focus on being in the right place and then making sure we are there consistently.

And that all comes down to choosing the right marketing channels and platforms.

In an ideal world, you'd be doing it all – ads, direct mail, email, all social media platforms, SEO and so on. In reality, you'd need a whole team and a huge budget to do it all, so unless you want to start hiring, you'll need to be selective.

In this section, we're going to look at some of the most common marketing tactics, and I'm going to give you the basics, so you can decide which you want to explore further.

Social media

Social Media is fab. It's free, it's easy to use, and you can reach a lot of people. But there are downsides too.

For example, it's very easy to focus on the wrong numbers – followers, likes, and views. These things are important, but you want to attract the right followers, not just any old followers, and you want those likes and views to translate into sales.

The good news is you can use social media to move prospects all the way through your funnel, from attracting them and nurturing them right through to converting them into customers or clients.

But, while using a single social media platform for every stage of the funnel is possible, don't rely on it as your only marketing tool. You could lose your account at any moment – the platform could cease to exist (whatever happened to Myspace), you could be banned or have your profile deleted, or the terms of use could change for no reason.

That's why it's always good to have a backup plan. I recommend having a website as a minimum – at least then, people can still find you if you disappear from their favourite platform. An email list is also a good idea as you'll be able to let your followers know if you are temporarily (or permanently) blocked from a particular platform.

What should you post about?

As with any content you are creating, you need to keep your end goal in mind – attracting the right clients. There's nothing wrong with sharing the odd post just for fun, but don't lose sight of why you are there. You're trying to attract clients, not fans.

I recommend creating a mix of three main types of content: content to help you increase reach, content to help you establish your expertise, and content to promote your services.

Increase reach

There's no point posting on social media if you only have three followers, so you'll want to grow your audience. And ideally, you want to grow it with people who might go on to buy your products or services.

Posts that start conversations, posts about personal experiences, and posts that are entertaining help you get engagement, which in turn helps you increase your reach and attract new followers. You can also optimise your content using hashtags (or the equivalent on your chosen social platform).

Establish expertise

You can build trust and credibility by establishing your expertise. Don't just tell people how good you are – show them.

This can be done by sharing tips and advice. Or by sharing case studies and testimonials.

Promote services

The final (and probably most important type of content) is promotional content. It's no use building a huge audience if nobody knows what you do.

Your promotional posts should talk about the problems you solve. They should also push people to the next stage of your process – subscribe to your emails, buy your thing, join your group, book your event, or click through to your website, etc.

Don't focus on vanity metrics

Content designed to increase reach will always get more views than informational or promotional content – that's the point of it.

Personal stories, entertaining content, and conversation starters appeal to a wider audience. If I share a picture of a cute puppy, it'll get a lot of likes because a lot of people like cute puppies.

The danger with this type of content is that you can get addicted to likes and views. So you start creating more and more entertaining and engaging content and less promotional content.

Don't fall into this trap.

Build your audience and attract new followers, then post about the problems you solve so you can get potential buyers into your marketing funnels.

Use social media as a marketing tool. To generate enquiries. To drive traffic to your website. To get email subscribers. To promote your services.

Yes, it can be a great place to learn, find suppliers, and even make new friends, but they should be happy consequences, not your primary focus.

You can use social media for those things, but don't kid yourself that it's productive or constructive.

If you aren't getting conversions from your social media activity, it's not helping you build your business.

Email

Email is another fantastic marketing tool – it's free to use, and most people have an email address.

And with so many affordable options for automating your emails, it makes sense to build a subscriber list.

You can then nurture your subscribers and move them through your marketing process.

Lead magnets and nurture sequences

There are a lot of marketing terms I hate, and lead magnet is one of them. But as much as I dislike the term, I love the concept.

Your lead magnet is your gingerbread house. It's something that appeals to your ideal clients.

And in exchange for you giving it to them, they give you their email address.

You then follow up on your lead magnet with a series of emails to build interest, desire, trust, and credibility.

Your lead magnet could be anything – a PDF guide, a checklist, a free trial, a webinar, a book, a quiz, or information.

The only stipulation is it has to be something your ideal clients are prepared to exchange their email addresses for.

Most of us understand that when we sign up for something that requires our email address, we will probably get some marketing emails.

And as long as our data isn't being sold and we can unsubscribe from those emails, we're usually ok with it.

But that doesn't mean we want to receive five emails within fifteen minutes of subscribing.

A surefire way to get readers to hit that unsubscribe button is to bombard them with a load of sales pitches before they've even had a chance to check out the thing they originally signed up for.

You don't need to go straight in for the kill.

You wouldn't ask someone to marry you on the first date, so don't rush things with your new prospects.

Woo them.

It's called a nurture sequence because that's what you're trying to do – nurture your readers. Establish your credibility, gain their trust, and show them how you can improve their life or business.

How many emails you need to send will depend on several factors, not least the level of commitment you're asking for. Booking a free discovery call or buying a £15 product is a much lower risk than signing up for a £10k package.

The great thing about emails is you can test different sequences and measure the results to see which works best.

Subscriber lists and newsletters

You don't have to create a lead magnet to build a subscriber list. Some people will sign up to your list to receive offers and updates, regular newsletters, or useful content.

You can send tips, advice, links to your latest blog posts, updates about new products, industry news, or entertaining content. And you can send emails daily, weekly, monthly, or just whenever you have something interesting to say.

But let subscribers know what to expect, give them the option to unsubscribe at any time, and don't only email them when you want something.

I've subscribed to too many email lists where you only hear from the company when they want your money. If you're going to build a subscriber list, be consistent – stay in touch with your subscribers all year round, not just when you've got a new product you want to sell.

Your website

If you don't already have a website, I recommend getting one. It doesn't have to be fancy – there are loads of affordable 'build your own' options.

I recommend having a website because you have full control over it. If you're using a single social media platform for marketing, what happens if you get banned, the platform changes its rules, or it ceases to exist? You have to start again. If you have a website, you don't have this problem.

And your website can be designed to suit you. It can be whatever you want it to be – a shop, a brochure, a lead generation tool, a content library, a knowledge base, a client portal, a membership site. It's entirely up to you.

It's designed to suit your business – you don't have to worry about algorithms or content restrictions – visitors see what you want them to see.

A website alone won't get you clients

While I recommend having a website, it's important to understand that building a website won't suddenly make clients appear.

I've lost track of the number of times I've seen people invest more money than they should into a fancy new website, only to be baffled when they don't suddenly have an influx of enquiries. And when the enquiries don't come flooding in, they blame the web designer, the copywriter, or the marketing agency.

And then there are the people who already have a decent site, but it doesn't bring any enquiries in, so they invest a load more money to get a new one built. And still, all they get is tumbleweed.

Why?

Because websites are not magic.

There are two crucial things you need to do if you want your website to get results:

- Get people to your website
- Get people to take action when they visit your website

Remember my basic marketing process, attract, nurture, convert?

Well, it applies to your website – attract people to it, nurture them while they're there, then convert them into enquiries, subscribers, or buyers.

Your website is a marketing tool – a way to move people to the next stage of your marketing process.

Attracting people to your website

If you want to drive traffic to your website, you need to do more than just stick the address on your business card and add the links to your social media accounts.

You need to give people a reason to visit.

You can do this by making sure you get found by people searching for what you offer. This is where SEO and paid search come in.

Or you can entice people to your site with great content – blogs, videos, podcasts, etc.

Or you can create persuasive sales copy that convinces people to click through to your site so they can find out more about you, subscribe to your emails, or make a purchase.

Keeping your visitors interested

Once you've got your ideal prospects on your website, you want to keep their attention. This will come down to your copy.

One of the biggest mistakes people make with their website is making it all about them.

Your website should be about your ideal clients.

We've already looked at interest, desire, trust, and credibility. Keep these elements in mind when you're writing your website copy.

If you put something on the page, ask yourself:

Will this generate interest in what I offer?

Will this create a desire to buy from/work with me?

Will this help me build trust with my ideal clients?

Will this help me establish my credibility?

If the answer is no to all four questions, you need to consider why you are including it on the page.

Talk about the problems you solve, the outcomes you deliver, and the benefits of working with you over anybody else.

Show you can be trusted to deliver, and demonstrate your expertise and credibility.

Notice how I use the words 'show' and 'demonstrate' rather than tell?

You can tell people you are brilliant at what you do, but they are more likely to believe you if you show them.

Use case studies or client feedback to back up your claims.

Getting visitors to take action

Your website is a stepping stone, not necessarily the final destination.

If you sell products through your website, your goal will be to get sales.

But if you don't sell directly through your site, everything on there should be geared towards getting people to take the next step.

What action do you want them to take?

Subscribe to your email list?

Book a call?

Request a quote?

Focus on getting visitors to the next stage of the process. Don't oversell your big-ticket item.

I don't sell my mentoring programme through my website. I focus on the problems I can solve and then get potential clients to make low-cost or low-risk commitments.

I mention mentoring and share client feedback, but I'm not asking for the sale.

My mentoring programme requires an investment of time, money, and effort, so I want to build trust first. I want my potential clients to feel like they know me and understand what would be involved before they make that commitment.

If you sell high-ticket packages, don't focus on getting commitment for these through your website. Focus on getting a low-cost, low-risk commitment, such as booking a call or submitting a quote request.

Talk about the problems you solve and get readers to take the next step.

Don't make your website about you

"Welcome to my website"

If the first line on your home page reads something like the above, change it today.

It's a nice sentiment – perfectly pleasant. But it's also a wasted opportunity.

When potential clients land on your home page, they want to know whether you offer what they need. They don't want to search for the answer. They want you to tell them straight away.

So rather than welcoming people to your website, tell them what you do, who you help, or why they should hang around.

"Exercise classes for busy mums"

"Accountancy services for salon owners"

"Email marketing for construction businesses"

These are all far better openers than a welcome message that tells readers absolutely nothing about you, the problems you solve, or the outcomes you deliver.

And don't "we" on your readers.

Some people have a weird tendency to talk extensively about themselves on their website:

*"**We** have over ten years of industry experience, and **we** are passionate about what **we** do. **We** offer a wide range of services, and **we** can tailor our support to suit the needs of any business. **We** are friendly, reliable and professional. **We** pride ourselves on delivering excellent service."*

We. We. We.

I refer to this as we-ing on people, and the problem is it's boring.

The same goes for "I".

*"**I** am experienced in this. **I** am passionate about that. **I** have this qualification. **I** have that certification. **I** am so boring."*

Stop talking about yourself.

Instead of "**we** offer XYZ", say, "**you** will get XYZ."

Be clear what action you want readers to take next

Readers expect you to tell them what the next step is, so don't leave them guessing. Make sure every page has a call to action.

If you want readers to book a call, make your call to action "book a call". If you want them to complete a contact form, tell them to complete the contact form.

Base your call to action on what is convenient to you.

If, like me, you don't take unscheduled calls, then don't put your phone number on your website or ask people to call you.

Your website is always a work in progress

Think of your website like a house. You don't move into a new house and keep it the same forever. You decorate, redecorate, update the carpets, and change the furniture – you might even remodel, add an extension, or convert the loft.

It should be the same with your website. Maintain and 'redecorate' it to stop it from getting old, tired and outdated.

Change the layout, test different call to actions, tweak the copy, add new testimonials, and update your blog.

You can do it a page at a time or all at once. But keep reviewing your site regularly to ensure it's accurate, up to date and looking good for your visitors.

Your business doesn't ever stay the same, nor should your website – think of it as a work in progress.

If you don't have control over your site content, get control. If your web agency doesn't let you update content, make layout changes, add pages, or add the functions you need to your site, switch to one that does.

Content marketing

I'm a huge fan of content marketing. I use it myself and have generated thousands of pounds in business by doing so.

But content marketing is not a quick fix. It takes time and patience.

Creating the content is only part of the process – you've got to get your content in front of people – and not just any people, the right people.

What is content marketing?

Before we get into how to do content marketing, let's take a look at what it actually is.

According to the Content Marketing Institute:

"Content marketing is a strategic marketing approach focused on creating and distributing valuable, relevant, and consistent content to attract and retain a clearly defined audience — and, ultimately, to drive profitable customer action."

There are five key points to this definition, so let's break them down in a little more detail.

Strategic

"Content marketing is a strategic marketing approach"

A common mistake I see people make with content marketing is focusing on the content part and not the marketing part. They just create content without thinking about who it is for or why they are creating it. They don't have a strategy.

It's too easy to put posts on social media and feel like you are making progress because you get lots of followers, likes and views. But if those followers, likes and views don't turn into profitable customer action, you're just wasting your time.

Likes and views are not conversions. Posting pictures of your dog will get you lots of engagement, but it's unlikely to lead to sales. Ignore the vanity metrics and focus on your objectives – attracting your ideal clients.

Your content should move people through a process from never having heard of you to becoming a customer.

Creating and distributing

Another mistake people make with content marketing is focusing on creation but not distribution. Sticking a blog post on your website won't magically generate a hundred new leads overnight – it just doesn't work like that.

It's not a case of 'if you build it, they will come' – you have to let people know your content exists.

Social media and email are my favourite channels for distributing content, but you can also use paid ads, influencer marketing, or sponsored links – there are loads of ways to get your content out there.

Valuable, relevant, and consistent

Don't just create any old content and hope for the best. If you want your content to generate leads, you need to make it:

Valuable: it has to be something your ideal client wants – information, advice, or entertainment.

Relevant: it's got to be relevant to your audience – you don't want to attract the wrong people.

Consistent: don't just turn up when you want to sell something – be consistently visible.

Clearly defined audience

We've already covered the importance of knowing your ideal client – you've got to know who you're selling to. If you don't, creating relevant content will be much harder.

Drive profitable customer action

And now we're back to the main goal of any marketing, which is to sell. What's the point of building an audience, getting subscribers or driving traffic to your site if you are never going to turn any of those followers, subscribers, or website visitors into customers?

If you create content simply for the sake of creating content, you might get results, but you probably won't get the results you want.

Every piece of copy or content you create should serve a purpose – to attract clients into your funnel or to move them through it.

So before you create any content, answer these two questions:

What is the purpose of this content?

- Attract followers
- Attract email subscribers
- Establish trust and credibility
- Demonstrate your expertise
- Increase your reach
- Highlight the benefits of working with you
- Raise awareness around what you do
- Encourage repeat business/customer loyalty
- Keep in touch with existing customers to stay front of mind

- Repel the wrong type of customers
- Get found in searches
- Promote your products or services
- Provide evidence that you deliver on promises
- Generate leads/enquiries
- Make a sale

What do you want the reader to do once they have read/viewed this content?

- Follow you/connect with you on social media
- Click through to your website
- Subscribe to an email series/newsletter
- Watch a video/read a blog post/listen to a podcast
- Book a call
- Download something
- Make an enquiry
- Sign up to an event
- Buy something

If you know the purpose of your content, it makes it easier to create the right kind of content.

Types of content

Different types of content will help you achieve different objectives.

I break content down into five key categories: entertaining, optimised, insightful/personal, informative, and promotional

Entertaining

The main purpose of entertaining content is to attract attention.

This sort of content is easy reading/listening/viewing. It can be amusing, shocking or interesting.

For example:

- 10 biggest wedding disasters
- 25 of the worst graphic design fails
- How an extra comma cost the US government $2 million
- Could you be breaking this obscure law without even realising it?

Sharing content like this on social media can help you increase your reach as it's the sort of content people will "like" or share. It can also help you get clicks through to your website.

But remember, likes and clicks are only useful if you can convert some of them into subscribers, followers, or buyers. So if you're creating content in this category, try and keep it related to what you do.

Optimised

On social media, you can optimise content with hashtags and tags.

With blog posts and videos, you can optimise your content for search engines by focusing on key search terms.

What questions are people typing into Google or YouTube?

- What's the difference between copywriting and content writing?
- Can you switch from sole trader to limited company?
- What are the best exercises for getting rid of bingo wings?

Create content around the things people are searching for.

Insightful/personal

This type of content gives people an insight into you or your company and can cover things like:

- Case studies
- Meet the team profiles
- Day in the life of a copywriter
- Company history
- Charity initiatives

If you're building a personal brand, you might share social media posts about your hobbies and interests or share some personal experiences.

Don't worry – you don't have to share your deepest darkest secrets or give details about your bowel movements. Just give your ideal clients an insight into what kind of person you are.

Informative

This type of content helps you demonstrate your expertise and establish credibility.

- Top tips/How to...
- Basic/beginner's/quick/ultimate guide to

- Latest industry/legislation changes – how could they impact your clients

What are your most frequently asked questions?

What common mistakes are your potential clients making?

Use these as ideas for your content.

You can also combine informative and optimised content by giving detailed answers to the questions people are typing into search engines.

Promotional

As well as social media posts to promote your products and services, you can create longer-form promotional content:

- 10 ways a virtual assistant can save you money
- How to choose your accountant
- Why every business owner should learn the basics of copywriting

Promotional content can cross over into informative content and optimised content so you can increase reach, establish your expertise, and promote your services in one.

Content format

All five types of content can be delivered in a huge variety of formats. And you can present the same content in several different formats to cater to different preferences.

- Blogs/articles
- Social media posts
- White papers/research papers
- Videos
- Podcasts
- eBooks/books/booklets
- PDFs
- Infographics/carousels
- Presentations
- Webinars
- Courses
- Emails
- Trials/demos

Go for evergreen over bandwagon content

There's always something in the news or some fad or trend that's getting a lot of attention, and it's easy to jump on the bandwagon and create content around it.

But, while writing a social media post about the biggest news story or the latest thing to go viral isn't hugely time-consuming, you don't want to waste hours creating detailed content around the subject.

These things get lots of attention and focus for a couple of days, maybe a couple of weeks, perhaps a month at a push.

But then they are gone, forgotten about, and everyone has moved on to the next thing.

And when that happens, you're stuck with a video or blog post that is no longer relevant, that can't be reused or repurposed anywhere, and that nobody is interested in anymore.

So instead of creating content about the latest craze, focus on creating content with longevity – content that can be used and reshared for months and even years to come.

Disposable content might get you a few extra views, but it will get forgotten about as quickly as the news story itself.

Create content people want to bookmark, save or share.

Go for quality over quantity

You don't need daily videos or blog posts to make content marketing work. Go for quality of content over quantity of content every time.

If you're creating rubbish content, it becomes like the boy who cried wolf – people will just stop paying attention to you.

So spend some time creating good content. Answer people's questions in depth. Provide value-adding advice. Share your expert insights or opinions on a subject.

Whether you are creating videos, podcasts, or written content, you want people to feel like watching, listening, or reading that content was a good investment of their time.

Mediocre content won't achieve that.

Play to your strengths

Not everyone is funny. Not everyone writes well. Not everyone is engaging on video.

So play to your strengths.

If you aren't entertaining, then be informative.

If you are awkward and uncomfortable on camera, then create written content or podcasts. Or film interview-style videos rather than selfie-style videos.

If you struggle to write, try using a dictation app and then tweaking what you've said. Or hire someone to turn your audio ramblings into blog posts for you.

People will tell you that you need to do this, that, and the other, but you don't have to do everything. You don't have to make any content at all if you don't want to – there are other forms of marketing.

So do what you're good at. If it's writing funny social posts, do that. If it's writing in-depth white papers, do that. If it's sharing your expertise and insight in short videos, do that.

Create content your ideal clients will be interested in

Sounds pretty obvious, but it's surprising how many people create content without thinking about their target audience.

Sure, sharing a video of your team doing the latest TikTok dance craze might get a lot of likes, but is it going to get you meaningful engagement? Probably not. So, before you rush off to write about whatever the latest industry trend is, take a minute to decide whether your ideal clients will actually be interested.

Social media is a great place to get ideas for content. You can ask people what they'd like you to cover in an article or video. You can test different content ideas on a small scale. And you can look at what type of content your target audience already engages with.

Check out your competitors' content and see which topics get the most interest – can you put an alternative spin on a subject or present it differently? Look at what your existing clients engage with. Find groups or hashtags your ideal clients follow and look at the questions and conversations that are going on.

And listen to people. What questions do you get asked over and over again? What advice do you find yourself repeating? What mistakes do you see people making? These could be great subjects for your next piece of content.

Don't try and appeal to everyone

The most important thing to remember when creating content is not to try to appeal to everyone. It's impossible, and it doesn't make for good content.

Instead, think about the sort of person you want to do business with – your ideal client – and write (or talk) as though you are writing for them (or speaking directly to them). The more your content resonates with someone, the more likely they are to want to do business with you.

Don't focus on likes and views – focus on conversions. If ten people see your content and one becomes a customer, that's better than 100 people seeing it and none of them becoming a customer.

Share your content and get others to share it

It's not enough to just stick a blog post or video on your website and hope your ideal clients will find it. You've got to get it out there in front of people.

Social media is the easiest way, and it's free. But don't just share a link or video with no context – explain why people should click through to your article or watch your video. What's in it for them?

As well as sharing content yourself, get other people to share it. If you have colleagues, they should be sharing it, but suppliers and clients might share too if it is useful to their audience.

And you don't have to only approach people you know. You might want to do some blogger outreach – the process of reaching out to other bloggers or journalists and asking them to link to or share your content.

If you have an email subscriber list or send out newsletters, include links to your latest blog posts or videos in your next email.

You could even include a link to your latest content in your email signature – it's far more interesting than just a link to your website homepage.

Reshare – don't just share your content once

Not everyone you are connected to will see your content the first time you share it. In fact, you'd be lucky if 20% of your followers saw it. And of those that do see it, not all of them will watch, read, or listen the first time around. So share your content multiple times. Reshare it on social media but try using different copy in the accompanying post.

Don't be scared of resharing content. Companies don't make a TV ad and only show it once. People are used to seeing the same things more than once – it's perfectly normal.

And as well as resharing on social media, link back to older content from new content or add a 'related content' section to your latest blog post.

Repurpose your content

Not everyone likes content in the same format. Some people like videos, while others prefer blog posts. Some people want to read a book, while others prefer audiobooks. Some people want short, easy-to-digest content, others want in-depth white papers.

The point is not everyone wants to view your content in the way you'd like them to view it.

So repurpose it.

Turn blog posts into videos and vice versa. Take sections of your blog posts and turn them into standalone social media posts. Turn old presentations into videos or blog posts. Turn an email series into a PDF. Create PDFs of any informational articles.

Once you have your content, make the most out of it.

Keep your goal in mind

It's too easy to get distracted by content marketing and start veering off course.

Keep your goal in mind and measure the right things.

Your content might be attracting people, but is it driving profitable action?

While you might be making lots of new friends on social media, are any of them turning into customers?

You might be getting lots of lovely clicks through to your website, but are any of the visitors buying?

Do your emails win you any business, or are you getting lots of unsubscribes once people have bagged themselves the freebie content?

If you are getting engagement with your content, but your sales aren't increasing, then it might be time to look closely at the audience you have built. Are they the right fit for your products and services? If not, you need to change your content to attract the right people.

And if you have attracted the right audience, but they aren't buying, then you need to look at why they aren't buying.

Is your website copy up to scratch – does it make it clear what you offer and why people should buy it? Does your website have clear call to actions, and is it easy for people to take those actions?

When you get email enquiries, are your responses well-written, or do they sound dull, generic and disinterested?

When people approach you on social media, are you too aggressive in your responses, or are you too laid back, not asking for the sale?

If your content isn't helping you attract, nurture and convert more of your ideal clients, you need to revise your content strategy.

SEO and paid search

I've lumped search engine optimisation (SEO) and paid search together because the idea behind both is the same – you want to get found when people are searching for what you offer.

The only difference is whether you are showing up in organic search results or you have paid to be found for specific keywords.

SEO and paid search are good ways of getting your message in front of people at the right time. If someone is searching for what you offer, they are usually already interested in it – they already have a need.

There are two ways you can utilise SEO and paid search.

You can get found when people are searching for your services:

- Accountant for small businesses
- Web designers in Manchester
- Finance recruitment
- Logo design for new business
- Business coach for construction companies

You would then have a landing page promoting this specific service.

You can get found for search queries relating to what you do:

- What should I include in a job ad?
- How long should a blog post be?
- How do I get ISO accredited?
- What is Agile?
- What makes a good logo?

You then create content that answers the question in detail and links to your products or services.

It's not all about written content

When you're using SEO or paid search for your marketing, you don't have to stick to written content.

Search engines like Google happily show videos in search results if the content is relevant.

It's also worth noting that at the time of writing this book, YouTube is the second biggest search engine after Google.

More and more people are choosing to get answers from videos rather than articles. So if written content isn't your thing, you can always create great video content instead.

Which is better organic SEO or paid search?

There are pros and cons to both.

Getting ranked organically can take longer, and algorithms are always changing, so all your hard work can quickly get undone.

Paid search can get results faster, but ranking for the most common keywords can be expensive.

Both SEO and paid search can be a huge waste of time and money if they aren't done well. If you're new to freelancing, there are better places to start. But if you do go down this route, learn the basics first or hire an expert.

If you want to go it alone, SEO involves less financial risk. You can do your own keyword research and create optimised content. But you'll also need to consider the technical aspects and how to get backlinks. Algorithms are constantly changing, so you need to keep on top of the latest updates.

Paid ads can get you to the top of the search results faster, but they require money – the clue is in the name. If you don't choose the right keywords (or you don't eliminate the wrong ones), you can end up out of pocket pretty quickly. So don't rush into this unless you are confident you know what you are doing or are working with someone who has proven results in this area.

Incorporating SEO into your content marketing strategy

If you don't want to invest time or money into SEO or paid ads, you can still incorporate some elements of SEO into your content marketing strategy.

Do basic keyword research to find out what your ideal clients are searching for and create great content around those topics.

After all, if people search those topics on Google, it stands to reason that some of your social media followers and email subscribers might also have questions about the same topics.

Optimising your blog posts whenever possible won't hurt your marketing, even if SEO isn't your main focus.

Direct marketing

Many freelancers steer clear of direct marketing because it feels too "salesy", but it shouldn't be dismissed too quickly.

Attracting clients to you can take time and patience. You're relying on your ideal clients looking for what you do, noticing you online, or stumbling across you by accident. Direct marketing can get you in front of your ideal clients much faster.

Let's say you're a window cleaner, and you cover certain postcodes. It doesn't make sense to spend hours writing blog posts about window cleaning in the hope someone who lives in one of the areas you cover sees them on Facebook. It would make more sense to put leaflets through the doors of houses in the areas you cover. The people who live in those houses are your ideal clients.

If you offer accounting services for property developers, you could run an ad in a magazine for property developers.

If you offer wedding photography, you could run Facebook ads targeting people who have recently gotten engaged within the locations you cover.

If you offer marketing services to IT businesses, you could contact owners or decision-makers in IT companies.

If what you offer is niche or has geographical constraints, then I'd definitely consider direct marketing.

One of the biggest advantages of direct marketing over indirect marketing is it can be much easier to track results. And you can test and measure different versions of an ad, email, or letter to see which gets the best response.

But if you go down the direct marketing route, take time to do it properly.

Cold outreach

Many people argue that cold outreach is dead – whether it's a cold call, a direct message on social media, or an emailed sales pitch.

I disagree.

I don't do cold outreach myself, but there are loads of businesses out there who still get sales from cold outreach, and I'm a huge advocate of cold outreach for certain businesses.

If you know exactly who your ideal clients are and you have something they need, why wouldn't you reach out to them directly?

The problem with cold emails or messages isn't that they don't work – it's that most of them are terrible.

Too many people opt for the spray and pray approach – send a generic email to as many people as possible and hope for the best.

But sending out generic sales pitches to anyone with an email address or social media account is akin to asking every person in a nightclub if they fancy some sexy time with you.

You might get lucky, but chances are, you won't. And you might even end up getting a few slaps.

Playing the numbers game is not a great strategy when it comes to marketing. A generic email allows you to hit up a large number of people quickly, but your conversions will likely be low. And think of the damage you could be doing to your reputation.

Most people can spot a generic and poorly researched email a mile off. It's lazy marketing.

And if you're lazy with your marketing, what else are you lazy with? The quality of your products and services maybe? It might be an incorrect assumption, but that doesn't mean people won't make it.

If you pitch to me and it's clear you haven't even bothered to do some basic research into me or my company, you're unlikely to hold my attention. Lines like "we've worked with businesses like yours" when you clearly have no idea what my business does just come across as insincere and dishonest.

And I could be your ideal client. Or I could have lots of clients that are your ideal clients. But you've put me off with your insincerity and laziness.

Playing the numbers game with your marketing doesn't make me feel like you value my business.

If you want better results from your cold outreach, put a little effort into researching your recipients and personalising your content.

At the very least, look over their website or social media pages to check if they match your ideal client profile.

And do not begin your messages by talking about yourself. Show your reader you understand them. Make your content about them and their needs, their challenges, and the outcomes you can deliver for them.

Alternatives to cold outreach

I know a lot of freelancers cringe at the idea of cold-pitching, so you'll probably be pleased to know there are other ways to do direct marketing. I'm not going to go into huge amounts of detail, but here are just a few examples:

Facebook Ads – targeted to very specific demographics.

Press Ads – placed in relevant publications.

Brochures – handed out at relevant events or mailed to potential clients.

Flyers – handed out at events, posted through doors or included in third-party packages.

Billboards – to get seen in areas where you do business.

Experiential marketing – attend trade shows, award ceremonies, exhibitions, events or festivals (or host your own) and create experiences, do demos or give out samples.

I've bought things myself after seeing an ad or getting a flyer through the door, so it is effective – something worth thinking about if you haven't considered it before.

Networking

I'm putting networking under direct marketing because, essentially, that's what it is.

You're going to face-to-face events to seek out your ideal client and start a conversation with them.

When you join referral networking groups, you are asking other members of your group to approach your ideal clients on your behalf. It's still direct marketing, just with a buffer in between.

Networking can be a good way to make connections, but it takes a lot of time, effort and patience to generate the right results.

You might get a lot of referrals, but some of them will be duds, some of them timewasters, and some of them not the type of clients you want.

Networking has its benefits, but there are more effective marketing strategies. As with any type of marketing, if it isn't getting results, don't keep investing time or energy into it.

Action time: Choosing your channels

There are multiple marketing methods, channels and platforms to choose from. All of them work for some people, but none of them work for everyone.

You need to figure out which are right for your business.

The first thing to do is think about which approach is most likely to get you in front of the right people.

What is the most effective way to reach your ideal clients?

Which platforms are your ideal clients most likely to be using?

What type of marketing is most likely to get their attention?

Another consideration should be how you can play to your strengths.

Are you a good writer?

Are you confident in front of a camera?

Are you happy to cold call?

Do you know how to write sales copy?

Have you already got a following on a specific social media platform?

Have you got great design skills?

Can you create video animations?

Find channels where you can utilise your existing skills or invest in developing areas where you already have a basic knowledge.

And don't put all your eggs in one basket. You don't want to spread yourself too thin with your marketing, but you also don't want to rely on one channel.

Which marketing channels and activities will help you reach your ideal clients and play to your strengths?

The story so far: Part eight summary

Key takeaways:

- If you want to be in front of your ideal clients at the right time, you need to be in the right place.
- Don't lose sight of your end goal – moving people towards a sale.
- Before creating any content, ask yourself what the purpose of the content is and what you want people to do after reading/viewing/listening.
- When doing cold outreach, personalise the message as much as possible and make it about the reader.
- You don't have to do every type of marketing but don't put your eggs in one basket either.

Action points:

- Decide which marketing channels and activities will help you reach your ideal clients and play to your strengths.

Coming up next:

- Investing in the right tools and support.

Part nine: Even heroes have help

Get the right support

Cinderella had a fairy godmother, Aladdin had a genie, and Snow White had seven dwarfs looking out for her.

Even heroes need a helping hand now and then.

When I first started in business, I tried to do everything myself.

If I didn't know how to do it, I'd read articles, sign up for freebie guides and courses, and look for free advice and tips.

I didn't need to hire a consultant or coach, pay for training or anything like that – better to figure it out myself and save a few pennies.

And so I muddled along. But even though I was making money, I couldn't get to that next stage.

I was still stuck in the feast or famine cycle. I was still jumping through hoops to win work that I wasn't even that excited about.

Then I realised I needed to invest in my business and myself. I reached out to people – people I knew could help me.

Some of them were people I had avoided approaching in the past because I thought they might be too expensive for me. Or they might think I was too small fry to work with. Or they might think my business was a bit shit.

And do you know what?

Their services weren't too expensive.

And they didn't think I was too small fry.

And they didn't judge me.

I got the support I needed and learnt stuff that helped me move my business forward. And I got a return on investment.

Working for yourself doesn't mean doing everything by yourself. You don't have to slay the dragon alone.

It's ok to ask for help.

Outsource stuff you can't do or don't want to do

You might think you can save a few quid doing everything yourself, but something you thought would be relatively easy can end up taking hours of your time. Hours that would be better spent doing paid client work.

If something costs £100 to outsource, but the time it saves means you can earn £200, it's a no-brainer.

I've engaged the services of graphic designers, videographers, and animators because my design skills are terrible. I know I could never do as good a job as the people I hired, even if I spent a year trying.

How can you expect people to see the value in investing in your skills if you don't see the value in investing in other people's skills? Practice what you preach.

Don't overload yourself

Hopefully, after reading this book, you won't overload yourself with more work than you can handle, but if you do find yourself in that position, you've got decisions to make.

If it's a one-off, manage it and don't let it get out of hand again.

But if it's happening regularly, you need a long-term fix.

You can hire employees or use subcontractors. I've done both myself, and I wouldn't say one is better than the other – it's entirely up to you to decide which option works for your business. There are pros and cons to each.

Some people don't want to manage employees. They don't want the pressure of finding a salary for someone else every month. Other people want to grow a team and create jobs.

Some people prefer subcontracting work so they can scale the support up and down as required. Others don't trust subbies to do as good a job.

If you'd prefer not to go down either route, you need to up your prices and be more selective about the work you take on.

You can always find referral partners – people you'd recommend to anyone you can't or don't want to help. You might even be able to negotiate a finder's fee or commission.

Bring in the experts

I pay for managed IT services. I have an accountant to take care of all my tax returns. When I needed subcontractor agreements, I got them drawn up by a specialist.

Why? Because those people are experts in their industries, and I'm not.

It amazes me how often I see freelancers getting legal or financial advice from Facebook groups instead of speaking to someone who actually knows what they are doing.

There are experts and consultants in every field – marketing, sales, HR, finance, IT, legal, H&S.

Use those experts when you need them.

Get the right tools

You can wash your clothes in the sink, but most people have a washing machine.

You can sweep your floors with a dustpan and brush, but most people have a vacuum cleaner.

We'll happily invest in things to make our personal lives easier or more comfortable, so why wouldn't we do the same in our business?

And yet, when it comes to paying for support, training, personal development, tools or software, business owners are reluctant to make even the smallest investments.

I'm not saying you should throw money at things for fun – of course you need to be sensible, especially when it's a larger investment.

And I know money can be tight when you're a freelancer. You have to be careful what you spend when you don't know how much you will earn from one month to the next.

But don't scrimp on the things you need. Don't make life harder for yourself or your clients just to save a few pennies.

If you want people to take you seriously, you need to show you are serious about your business.

Let's talk about email

There's no reason to be using @hotmail or @yahoo email addresses. If you've got a domain name for your website, you can get a professional email address. If you look like a proper business, you're more likely to be treated like one.

And if you want to start an email subscriber list, don't just opt for the cheapest automation software – find one that does what you need. If a freebie version is a good fit, great. If it's not, invest a little.

Pay for the software you need

If there's a piece of software that improves your business, don't try and make do with the free version if you need the paid version.

During the pandemic in 2020, a lot of people started using Zoom to do video meetings. The free version had a 40-minute limit on sessions which wasn't ideal as most businesses were used to doing hour-long meetings.

But even though it was less than £10 a month to upgrade to unlimited meeting times, some business owners would get around the 40-minute limit by creating two separate meetings for what was really a single meeting.

I was doing a lot of 90-minute consultations and online training at the time. Can you imagine how crappy it would look to my clients if I made them log in and out of

Zoom every 40 minutes, just so I could save £100 a year? Especially when they were paying me more than that for the training session.

There are loads of fantastic and extremely affordable tools available that can help make your business more efficient. Don't be scared of making sensible investments.

Make it easy for clients to pay you

I know freelancers who won't set up GoCardless, Stripe, or Paypal for business because they don't want to pay commission fees.

They won't make it easier for clients to pay them because they don't want to miss out on what probably works out at less than a fiver per invoice. Just add an extra 2% to your price if it's that much of a big deal.

And invest in some accounting software. I use Xero myself, but there are plenty to choose from. You can use it to create and send professional-looking invoices, which can also link to Stripe for easy payment. And you can automatically send reminders when invoices are overdue.

It saves you admin time and helps you manage your bookkeeping more easily.

Invest in yourself

You'd get training and development opportunities if you worked for a company. There'd be people you could learn from, get support from, and ask for advice.

You shouldn't miss out on training and development just because you work for yourself.

I'm not suggesting you blow all your savings flying to training events around the world, but invest in the stuff that will help you get where you want to be.

At the very least, you should stay up to date with what's happening in your industry so you can deliver accurate, relevant advice and a great service to your clients.

There are loads of free and low-cost options – sign up for newsletters, read blogs, articles and books, subscribe to industry magazines or publications, watch videos or listen to podcasts.

And don't just invest in learning about your industry – learn stuff that will help you in your business.

Go to events, attend seminars, take training courses.

If you want to learn how to get the most from a specific social media platform, find a training course. If you want to be more assertive, do an assertiveness course.

Get bespoke support – a lot of experts offer strategy sessions, consultations, or power hours. These can be a cost-effective way of getting actionable advice without committing to long-term support.

But if you do want ongoing support, guidance, and accountability, consider working with a coach or mentor.

I mentor people. I have a mentor. And my mentor has a mentor.

Having someone in your corner giving you that support, holding you accountable, and sharing their knowledge and experience can be invaluable.

I wish I hadn't been so stubborn when I started my business. I wish I'd gotten support sooner.

Trying to pretend everything is going swimmingly when you feel like you're treading water is exhausting.

It's ok to admit you're struggling, some of your clients are frogs, and you don't love every minute of running your business

Find someone you can admit those things to – ideally, someone who has been where you are now and knows how to move forward. Someone who has the type of business you'd like to have.

Whatever training or support you invest in, make sure you implement the learnings.

If you're doing self-paced courses, it's up to you to self-motivate and actually do the work.

If you're doing instructor-led (either as a group or one-on-one), you'll have someone holding you accountable.

Set yourself a budget for learning and development, and don't be scared to invest in yourself to make your business better so you can better serve your clients.

Action time: Where do you need to invest?

Make a list of all the tasks you can't do or don't want to do – which of these could you outsource?

How can you stop overloading yourself with work? Will you hire employees, use subcontractors, increase your prices, niche down, or create self-serve products for your clients?

What software or tools do you need to make life easier for you or your clients?

Which areas of your business do you need more support with?

Which skills do you need to develop or build on?

How much are you going to invest in your learning and development over the next year?

You don't have to go on a spending spree today but look at which areas of your business would benefit from some investment within the next few months.

Where do you need to invest?

The story so far: Part nine summary

Key takeaways:

- You don't have to do everything alone – even fairytale heroes have a trusty sidekick.
- Outsource the things you can't do or don't want to do – utilise experts.
- You'll get where you want to be faster if you have people helping you get there.
- Invest in tools that will help you create a better business.
- Set a budget for your learning and development.

Action points:

- Decide what support, tools and training you need to move your business forward.

Coming up next:

- Your next steps.

Part ten: And they all lived happily ever after

It's over to you

As I said at the start of this book, only you can change the direction of your business.

You can get help and support to do it, but you've got to be prepared to put in the work and take responsibility for the success of your business.

You don't have to put up with shitty clients.

You don't have to deal with timewasters.

You don't have to accept low-paid work.

You can create a business that gives you your happy ever after.

Here's a reminder of how to do it.

Decide what your happy ever after looks like

If you skipped this part, do it now. You must have been thinking about it while reading this book, so you'll have some idea of what you want your life and business to look like.

What kind of work would you be happy to wake up to every day?

What kind of clients would be a joy to work with?

What would your ideal working week look like?

Do you dream of a team, or are you happy as a lone wolf?

What side projects would you love to work on when you've freed up the time?

Some people like to create vision boards or dream boards – a collage of images, affirmations, quotes, pictures, postcards, or other sources of inspiration. It's not something I use personally, but if it helps you stay focused on the goal, go for it.

Do what works for you.

Stick to the path

You know what you are working towards, so focus on that.

Don't get sidetracked or distracted by things that don't align with your goal.

When a new enquiry comes in, don't rush into saying yes. Think it through.

Is this the kind of work I want to do?

Is this the kind of client I want to work with?

Can I give this project my best?

It's fine to take on projects outside your usual scope if it is something that excites you.

But don't get tempted into taking on stuff you won't enjoy or won't be good at just because it's got a nice payday attached.

Tell yourself better stories

You are good enough.

You can do it.

It will work for you.

Stop getting in the way of your own success.

Forget what other people are doing and focus on what you're doing – creating your happy ever after.

Build your house out of bricks

If you've been completing the tasks throughout this book, you should have set your rules – your non-negotiables.

Your rules should be designed to help you create your happy ever after. They should be things you can control. And they should be things you will stick to.

Don't make rules if you're going to cave every time you get a little pushback.

Be strong.

Trust me – it is possible to build a business that works on your terms.

Value yourself

If you don't value your time and expertise, you can't expect anyone else to.

Set your prices based on the value you deliver and stand by them.

If other people don't like your prices, that's their problem, not yours.

And don't work for free.

You can make exceptions to this if you choose. For example, if you want to offer your services to a charity for free or you want to offer free discovery calls. But the key word here is "choose" – it's a choice you are making.

Don't feel pressured into giving your time for free. And have systems in place so you don't end up on pointless calls or in meetings with timewasters.

Personally, I'd steer clear of offering free calls unless you have a process for making sure those calls translate into high conversion rates.

Focus your marketing

Remember, the key to marketing is getting the right message in front of the right people at the right time.

Focus on attracting your ideal clients. Make all your marketing about them. For every marketing activity you do, ask yourself:

Who is this aimed at? What is the purpose? What action do I want them to take next?

For every advert, email, message, and piece of content you create, ask yourself:

- Will this generate interest in what I offer?
- Will this create a desire to buy from/work with me?
- Will this help me build trust with my ideal clients?
- Will this help me establish my credibility?

If the answer isn't yes to at least one of the above, question why you are creating that piece of content.

Get the right support

You don't have to do everything alone.

Get yourself a trusty sidekick or a fairy godmother – someone who can get you where you want to be.

If you need specialist advice or support, invest in an expert. If you need to develop your skills in an area, invest in training. If you need someone to guide you and hold you accountable, invest in a mentor.

And get the tools you need to make your business run efficiently. Don't compromise on quality just to save a few quid.

Setting targets

You've set your rules – your non-negotiables, but now we need some targets.

Targets are different to rules because you don't have control over them.

If you say, "I'm not going to answer client calls after 6pm", you can control that – you just don't answer the phone after 6pm.

But if you say, "I want five new clients per month", that's a target. You can't control it.

You can put steps in place to make it happen, but you have no control over whether you even get five enquiries a month, let alone whether they convert into clients or not.

So what's the point of setting targets if you can't control them?

Well, it's simple. Targets make things happen.

Think back to my first half marathon. I set a target of completing it in under two hours, but I didn't have control. I could have suffered an injury that meant I had to pull out, or I could have been ill on the day.

But if I hadn't set that target, I wouldn't have trained in the same way, and I wouldn't have achieved my goal.

I had a target to work towards and did everything within my control to achieve it.

You can do the same with targets in your business. You can set them and do everything within your control to achieve them.

If you want to win five new clients per month, you can implement processes to help you do it. Look at your conversion rates. How many enquiries convert into paying customers?

If it's 50%, then you need ten enquiries per month to get your five new clients. How are you going to generate those ten enquiries?

If you have a target of writing one blog post per month, how will you achieve that? How long does it take you to research, write, edit, and proofread a blog post? When can you block out time in your calendar to do it?

If you have a target of spending no longer than three hours a week on social media, how will you make sure you stick to that? Will you pre-write a bank of posts to save time? How long will you dedicate to replying to comments? How long will you spend searching for new connections?

You might not be able to achieve all your targets every week or month, but you're more likely to get close if you know what you're aiming for.

Break big goals down and set milestones

Let's say you've read this book and have decided you want to create a PDF guide to use as a lead magnet so you can build an email list.

Break the goal down into manageable chunks. What are you going to need?

- The guide itself
- A sign-up page
- An email sequence
- Email automation software
- A way to get people to the sign-up page

Now set a deadline for when you want to achieve your goal – I want to have it live by X date.

Then set yourself mini targets – finish the first draft of the guide by x date, write the copy for the sign-up page by x date, etc.

How much time will you need to set aside each day or week to work on each of your mini targets and meet your deadline? Schedule the time in your diary and stick to it.

Action time: What are your next steps?

Time to set yourself an action plan.

What do you want to achieve in the next 30 days, the next 90 days, or the next 12 months? What are your next steps?

Make your targets specific – "get more clients" and "charge more" are not specific.

- Increase prices by X%
- Learn how to...
- Get training on...
- Invest in...
- Rewrite website copy
- Start an email list

What are your monthly marketing or sales targets?

- 50 new email subscribers per month
- Post on social media three times per week
- Publish one new blog post a month
- Win three new clients per month

- Earn £X per month

Just like your rules, your targets should be designed to help you achieve your happy ever after.

What are your targets for the next 90 days?

The story so far: Part ten summary

Key takeaways:

- Focus on your happy ever after – don't get distracted from your goal.
- Stick to your non-negotiable rules and value yourself.
- Keep your marketing focused on your ideal clients.
- Rules are things you can control; targets give you something to work towards.
- Your rules and targets should be designed to help you achieve your happy ever after.

Action points:

- Set yourself goals and milestones for the next 90 days and beyond.

The sequel

What next?

Fairytales shouldn't need sequels – after all, everyone lives happily ever after, right?

But Disney has made a killing from fairytale sequels so they must be on to something, and I'm not about to question their success.

You might have reached the end of this book, but your story doesn't end here.

You now have three choices.

1. Ignore everything you've learned and carry on as you are.

2. Take some or all of the ideas from this book and start implementing changes to get where you want to be.

3. Get help and support from someone who will help you achieve your happy ever after.

What are you going to do?

Working with me

I work with freelancers, coaches, consultants, and service providers who feel frustrated.

Frustrated by not doing work they enjoy, not getting the clients they want, and not charging the prices they deserve.

If that sounds like you, then let me help you.

I've been there. I remember exactly how that frustration felt. Why was everyone else "smashing it" while I was working my arse off for clients who didn't appreciate me?

But now? Now I'm happier than I've ever been.

I want to help other people achieve that too. It's why I wrote this book.

And if you were to go away and put the stuff you've learned from this book into action, you would get results.

But I can't give you bespoke advice through a book. And there's only so far generic advice will get you, especially if you are trying to implement it alone.

When we work together one-on-one, I can give you bespoke advice. Plus, I will hold you accountable so you get where you want to be faster.

But there's only one of me, so I can't take on unlimited one-to-one clients. It's why I only work with people I feel confident I can help.

And because I don't just work with any Tom, Dick, or Harry, there are some criteria you need to meet before you consider working with me:

- **You must have an ethical business** – I do not work with scammers, con artists, or immoral people. If your success is based on screwing other people over, I don't want to hear from you.

- **You must have full control of your business and marketing** – if you are an MLM or a franchisee with restrictions on your marketing, pricing, or products, then I'm not right for you.

- **You must be prepared to put in some work** – working with me involves an investment of time, money, and effort, and it will only pay off if you are prepared to do what needs to be done.

- **You must be willing to try new things** – nothing kinky, I promise, but I might ask you to do things you've never tried before, so you'll need an open mind.

- **You must have a sense of humour** – ok, this one's not strictly essential, but it's definitely desirable because I want our time together to be fun as well as productive.

What my clients say

I'd like to think if you've got this far in the book, you know I'm not a big old bullshitter, and I can help you get results.

But if you are still unsure whether you can trust me, here are just some of the comments I've had about my one-to-one support.

"Lisa is very generous in sharing her knowledge and insights and was able to help me explain the transformation I can offer my clients in a very clear authentic fashion. Lisa didn't just give me a bit of training she gave me a new purpose and direction to my business as she really made me think about who my client is, their problems, and the solutions I have to offer." - Karen

"Supportive, Engaging, Motivating, Encouraging and Delivering are five words that sum up my experience of working with Lisa. I signed up for Lisa's 12 week course after searching for someone to support me and help drive business forward. From the very start I never questioned that decision. And, during this time I have learned how to write better copy, improve my marketing, increase my profits and boost my confidence. If you're looking for similar support contact Lisa. You won't regret it." - Peter

"I borrowed Lisa's brain for 90 minutes, but the information will last a lifetime. Lisa put me at ease with her down-to-earth nature and didn't flinch when I asked some really basic questions. If you want to make your business better, give Lisa your money." - Jac

"Incredible. I initially worked with Lisa on her 12 week course. She took me and a hotch-potch of enthusiasm, poor punctuation and a dodgy business model and enabled it to become consistent, credible and confident. Lisa continues to support my business, and I am bloody lucky to have Lisa in my corner helping me do the thing I love in a way that works for me." - Susie

About me

When you work with me, you get the best of me. Whether you book a single session or join my full mentoring programme, my goal is to give you as much value as possible in the time we have together.

I don't do fluff and nonsense – I do practical. I know some people like all the touchy-feely crap, but that's not my cup of tea. I'm not going to empower you or unlock your inner light or any of that bullshit. I'm going to give you actionable advice so you can get your business where you want it to be.

I'm straight-talking, honest and incredibly determined. I say it how it is, I'm a bit sweary, and I don't tolerate slackers. If that's likely to put you off, then maybe we aren't a good fit.

But if you don't mind hard work, aren't easily offended, and can handle some friendly sarcasm, then this could be the start of something special.

If you'd like my help and support, get in touch.

You can contact me via my website: www.makeyourcopycount.com

Or email me: lisa@makeyourcopycount.com

I look forward to helping you create your happy ever after.

•••••••••••

THANKS FOR READING

I hope you enjoyed The Freelance Fairytale: How to Create Your Happy Ever After.

I'd love to get your feedback on the book and hear what changes and actions you're implementing to help you get where you want to be.

You can email your feedback to lisa@makeyourcopycount.com and, as a thank you, I'll send you some bonus content.

Thanks again for reading – I look forward to hearing your thoughts.